Anonymous

Klers' Violin Repository of Dance Music

Vol. 1

Anonymous

Klers' Violin Repository of Dance Music
Vol. 1

ISBN/EAN: 9783337428150

Printed in Europe, USA, Canada, Australia, Japan

Cover: Foto ©Thomas Meinert / pixelio.de

More available books at **www.hansebooks.com**

[Book First.] KÖHLERS'

VIOLIN REPOSITORY

OF

DANCE MUSIC,

COMPRISING

Reels, Strathspeys, Hornpipes, Country Dances,

QUADRILLES, WALTZES, &c.

EDITED BY

A PROFESSIONAL PLAYER.

EDINBURGH: ERNEST KÖHLER & SON, MUSICSELLERS, 11 NORTH BRIDGE.
MORISON BROTHERS, 99 BUCHANAN STREET, GLASGOW.
MARTIN, ABERDEEN.   MENZIES & CO., EDINBURGH.
J. CUNNINGHAM, DUNDEE.   J. M. MILLER, PERTH.   WILLIAM DEAS, KIRKCALDY.
JAMES HORSBURGH, 73 GEORGE STREET, DUNEDIN, NEW ZEALAND.
LONDON: CATTY & DOBSON, 14 PILGRIM ST., LUDGATE HILL.

CONTENTS.

A S much of the spirit of Strathspey playing depends upon its peculiar bowing, a few examples are here given to illustrate and explain that style. Students requiring more minute explanations are referred to the work already alluded to,—*The Violin: How to Master it*, Chapter IX.

EXAMPLE OF ORDINARY DOTTED NOTES.

As they are written.

As they are played.

The second note of each group in the above example is detached with a smart jerk of the wrist in the same direction, thus giving the sharpness implied by the dot under the slur.

EXAMPLE OF DRIVEN NOTES.

LADY MARY RAMSAY (2nd part).

Sometimes played thus, with a bow to each note, when there is a danger of so expending the bow that it gets too near the heel.

But generally played thus by good players—

EXAMPLES OF THE DRIVEN NOTE FOLLOWED BY THREE NOTES LINKED ON TO ONE BOW.

TULLOCHGORUM.

MONYMUSK.

EXAMPLE OF THE LINKING OF DOTTED NOTES TO A CROTCHET.

THE "GARB OF OLD GAUL," or 42nd Highlanders' Quick Step.

Last time.

JIG. *Slower.*

Lively.

MRS. DONALDSON'S STRATHSPEY.

Slowly.

KÖHLERS' "VIOLIN REPOSITORY," 11 NORTH BRIDGE, EDINBURGH.

5

MISS MONTGOMERIE'S REEL.

OOR AULD GUDEMAN IS NOO AWA' (Strathspey).

LADY CATHCART'S STRATHSPEY.

MISS POLE'S REEL.

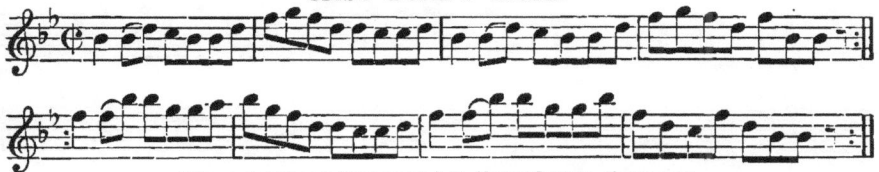

6

THE MERRY MASONS' MARCH (2nd Set).

Lively.

THE BANKS OF ALLAN WATER.

Slowly if not danced. **MRS. DUFF'S RECOVERY STRATHSPEY.**

7

MISS BUSHBY MAITLAND'S REEL.

MRS. M'LEOD OF ELANREOCH'S STRATHSPEY.

ATHOL BROSE.—Strathspey.

JENNY'S BAWBEE.—Reel.

KÖHLERS' "VIOLIN REPOSITORY," 11 NORTH BRIDGE, EDINBURGH.

THE HIGH LEVEL.

Fine.

1st time. *2nd time.*

Da Capo. E.

FACTORY SMOKE.

THE HOP BITTERS. *Arranged by* W. B. LAYBOURN.

KÖHLERS' "VIOLIN REPOSITORY," 11 NORTH BRIDGE, EDINBURGH.

MARQUIS OF LORNE.—Hornpipe.

RIGHTS OF MAN HORNPIPE.

PRIZE JIG.   *Arranged by* W. B. LAYBOURN.

THE BRIDAL MARCH.

With brilliance.   D. KIPPEN.

CORNET SOLO.

Da Capo.

OUR NATIVE HOME.

Quick March.   D. KIPPEN.

The *Lines* and *Two Dots* above (.—.) in *March* and *Quick March* indicate two up or down *Bows.*
KÖHLERS' "VIOLIN REPOSITORY," 11 NORTH BRIDGE, EDINBURGH.

STEWART'S LASSIE.—Strathspey.

NOTHING WILL YE TAK', MAN.—Reel.

MAJOR GRAHAM.—Strathspey.

LOCH TURRET.—Reel (1748). *Arranged by* W. B. LAYBOURN.

The *Lines* and *Two Dots* above (‿ ‿) in the *Strathspeys* indicate two up or down *Bows*.

KÖHLERS' "VIOLIN REPOSITORY," 11 NORTH BRIDGE, EDINBURGH.

GEBURSTAG'S VALSE.

The sign (‿) indicates two down or up *Bows*.

KÖHLERS' "VIOLIN REPOSITORY," 11 NORTH BRIDGE, EDINBURGH.

JULIANNU'S MARCIO GALLOP. *Arranged by* W. B. LAYBOURN.

The sign (⌣——⌣) indicates two down or up *Bows*.   ⊓ Down Bow, ⋁ Up Bow.

KÖHLERS' "VIOLIN REPOSITORY," 11 NORTH BRIDGE, EDINBURGH.

HORNPIPE.

TOM HANDFORD'S HORNPIPE.

THE FORTH BRIDGE.—Hornpipe. *Composed by* W. B. LAYBOURN.

15

Da Capo. E.

Introduction, Moderato. **LOVE NOT.—Quickstep.** *Arranged by* W. B. LAYBOURN.

KÜHLERS' "VIOLIN REPOSITORY," 11 NORTH BRIDGE, EDINBURGH.

1. ## ORIGINAL SET OF MAZURKAS. *Arranged by* W. B. LAYBOURN.

(To be continued.)—No. 8, November 1.

KÖHLERS' "VIOLIN REPOSITORY," 11 NORTH BRIDGE, EDINBURGH.

3. MAZURKAS—Continued. Polka for Finales. *Arr. by* W. B. LAYBOURN.

D.C. E.

4.

D.C.

∨ Up Bow. ⌣ Two Up or Down Bows.

KÖHLERS' "VIOLIN REPOSITORY," *Post Free,* 4½d.

1.

THE GREAT EASTERN,—Strathspey.

Six Reels and Strathspeys composed by A. W. Doig.

Segue Reel.

2.

GREAT EASTERN.—Reel.

Arranged by W. B. LAYBOURN.

D.C. Fine.

3.

BOB JOHNSTONE'S STRATHSPEY.

Segue Reel.

∨ Up Bow. ⌐⌐⌐ Two Up or Down Bows.

KÖHLERS' "VIOLIN REPOSITORY," 11 NORTH BRIDGE, EDINBURGH.

19

BOB JOHNSTONE'S REEL.

D.C. Fine.

ORR BRIGG.—Strathspey.

Segue Reel.

LOCHTY BLEACHERS.

D.C. Fine.

∨ Up Bow.   ⌣ Two Up or Down Bows.
KÖHLERS' "VIOLIN REPOSITORY," 11 NORTH BRIDGE, EDINBURGH.

1.   **EDINBURGH REVIEW WALTZES.**   *Composed by* P. MILNE.

2.

∨ Up Bow.   ⌣ Two Up or Down Bows.   ⊓ Down Bow.

KÖHLERS' "VIOLIN REPOSITORY," *Post Free,* 4½d.

3.

Arranged by W. B. LAYBOURN.

D.C. Fine.

ᴠ Up Bow. ⊓ Down Bow. ╌╌ Two Up or Down Bows.
KÖHLERS' "VIOLIN REPOSITORY," 11 NORTH BRIDGE, EDINBURGH.

PORT A RHODICH.—Strathspey.

Segue Reel. D.C.

TIMOUR THE TARTAR.—Reel. *Arranged by* W. B. LAYBOURN.

D.C. *Fine.*

∨ Up Bow. ⊓ Down Bow.

KÖHLERS' "VIOLIN REPOSITORY," 11 NORTH BRIDGE, EDINBURGH.

TULLOCHGORUM.—Strathspey.

D.C. Segue Reel.

JOHNNY COPE.—Reel. *Composed by* W. B. LAYBOURN.

D.C. Fine.

REEL OF TULLOCH. *Arranged by* W. B. LAYBOURN.

V Up Bow.   ⊓ Down Bow.

KÜHLERS' "VIOLIN REPOSITORY," 11 NORTH BRIDGE, EDINBURGH.

1. LANCERS QUADRILLES. *Arranged by* W. B. LAYBOURN.

D.C.

2.

(To be continued.) D.C.

∨ Up Bow. ⌣ Two Up or Down Bows.

LANCERS QUADRILLES—Continued. [NO. 4.

3.

D. C:

4.

D.C.

5.

D.C. Fine.

∨ Up Bow. — Two Up or Down Bows.
KÜHLERS' "VIOLIN REPOSITORY," *Post Free*, 4½d.

PRETTY DICK.—Polka.

By the EDITOR.

By the EDITOR.

MERRY ELVES.—Schottische.

1st time. | 2nd time.

TRIO.

Legato.

D.C.

28

MRS. GIBB'S HORNPIPE.

Arranged by W. B. LAYBOURN.

THE ALSTON HORNPIPE.—For Clog Dance.

Arr. by W. B. LAYBOURN.

THE BOTTLE BANK.

Composed by JAMES HILL, *Newcastle.*
Arranged by W. B. LAYBOURN.

∨ Up Bow.

KÜHLERS' "VIOLIN REPOSITORY," 11 NORTH BRIDGE, EDINBURGH.

SPEED THE PLOUGH.

By JAMES MUIRHEAD, 1800.

MRS. TAFF, OR BANK'S HORNPIPE.

Arr. by W. B. LAYBOURN.

∨ Up Bow.   ⊓ Down Bow.

KÖHLERS' "VIOLIN REPOSITORY," 11 NORTH BRIDGE, EDINBURGH.

MEDI VALSE.

Arranged by W. B. LAYBOURN.

BLUE BONNETS.—Contre Dance.

v Up Bow.   ⊓ Down Bow.   ‿•‿ Two Up or Down Bows.

KÖHLERS' "VIOLIN REPOSITORY," 11 NORTH BRIDGE, EDINBURGH.

1.   # MASANIELLO QUADRILLES. *Arranged by* W. B. LAYBOURN.

2.

Volti subito. *D.C.*

∨ Up Bow.   ⊓ Down Bow.   ⌐∙—∙ Two Up or Down Bows.

3.

4.

(To be continued.)

D.C.

∨ Up Bow.   ⊓ Down Bow.   ‿ Two Up or Down Bows.

KÖHLERS' "VIOLIN REPOSITORY," 11 NORTH BRIDGE, EDINBURGH.

KÖHLERS' VIOLIN REPOSITORY.

No 5.]　　　　　PRICE 4D.　　　　　[COPYRIGHT.

5. MASANIELLO QUADRILLES—Continued. *Arranged by* W. B. LAYBOURN.

Fine. D.C.

SIR ROGER DE COVERLY.—Contre Dance.

1st.　　　　*2nd.*

D.C.

∨ Up Bow.　　⊓ Down Bow.　　◦——◦ Two Up or Down Bows.

KÖHLERS' "VIOLIN REPOSITORY," 11 NORTH BRIDGE, EDINBURGH.

Arranged by W. B. LAYBOURN. **WILLIAM TELL—Rondo.** ROSSINI.

ADELPHI POLKA.

Arranged by W. B. LAYBOURN.

ROYAL ALBERT, OR PRINCE OF WALES CONTRE DANCE.

∨ Up Bow. ⊓ Down Bow. ⌐•⌐• Two Up or Down Bows.

Köhlers' "Violin Repository," 11 North Bridge, Edinburgh.

WM. YOUNG'S BEST MALT.—Strathspey. *By* ALEX. DEAS.

FAVOURITE JIG. *By* ALEX. DEAS.

KOHLER'S "VIOLIN REPOSITORY," 11 NORTH BRIDGE, EDINBURGH.

STIRLING CASTLE.—Strathspey. *Arranged by* W. B. LAYBOURN.

Segue Reel.

HARVEST HOME.

D.C. Fine.

TRIUMPH.—Contre Dance.

| 1st time. | | 2nd time. | D.C. |

∨ Up Bow.

KÖHLERS' "VIOLIN REPOSITORY," 11 NORTH BRIDGE, EDINBURGH.

ST. VALENTINE'S GALOP.

Arranged by W. B. LAYBOURN.

Piano part, 3d.

v Up Bow. ⊓ Down Bow. _·_·_ Two Up or Down Bows.

KÖHLERS' "VIOLIN REPOSITORY," 11 NORTH BRIDGE, EDINBURGH.

1. AGNES SOREL QUADRILLES. *Arranged by* W. B. LAYBOURN.

Piano part, 3d.

∨ Up Bow.   ⊓ Down Bow.   ⌐⌐ Two Up or Down Bows.
KÖHLERS' "VIOLIN REPOSITORY," 11 NORTH BRIDGE, EDINBURGH.

3.

4.

Piano part, 3d.   (To be continued.)   *D.C*

∨ Up Bow.   ⊓ Down Bow.   _·⎯·_ Two Up or Down Bows.

KÜHLERS' "VIOLIN REPOSITORY," 11 NORTH BRIDGE, EDINBURGH.

KÖHLERS' VIOLIN REPOSITORY.

No 6.]   PRICE 4D.   [COPYRIGHT.

5.   AGNES SOREL QUADRILLES—Continued.

Arr. by W. B. Laybourn.

PETRONELLA.—Contre Dance.

ᐯ Up Bow.   ⊓ Down Bow.   ⸱—⸱ Two Up or Down Bows.

Köhlers' "Violin Repository," 11 North Bridge, Edinburgh.

VICTORIA VALSE.

Arranged by W. B. LAYBOURN.

FIFE STRATHSPEY.

Composed by ALEX. DEAS.

D.C. Segue Reel.

MRS. SOUTAR OF PLAINS REEL.

By ALEX. DEAS.

D.C. Fine.

JAS. SOUTAR OF PLAINS JIG.

By ALEX. DEAS.

D.C. Fine.

∨ Up Bow.   ⊓ Down Bow.   ‑ ‑ ‑ Two Up or Down Bows.

KÜHLERS' "VIOLIN REPOSITORY," 11 NORTH BRIDGE, EDINBURGH.

THE 1st OF MAY.—Hornpipe.

Arr. by W. B. LAYBOURN.

THE TRUMPET HORNPIPE.

Arr. by W. B. LAYBOURN.

COLLEGE HORNPIPE, OR JACK'S THE LAD.

Arr. by W. B. LAYBOURN.

V Up Bow. ⊓ Down Bow.

KÜHLERS' "VIOLIN REPOSITORY," 11 NORTH BRIDGE, EDINBURGH.

CLASPER'S HORNPIPE.

Arranged by W. B. LAYBOURN.

DURHAM RANGERS' HORNPIPE.

Arranged by W. B. LAYBOURN.

THE JOCKEY DANCE.

Arranged by W. B. LAYBOURN.

∨ Up Bow.

KÖHLERS' "VIOLIN REPOSITORY," 11 NORTH BRIDGE, EDINBURGH.

THE BEAUTIES OF THE NORTH.—Strathspey. By FRASER.
Arranged by W. B. LAYBOURN.

D.C. *Segue Reel.*

THE NOVELTY REEL.
Arranged by W. B. LAYBOURN. By FRASER.

Fine.

HIGHLAND WHISKY.—Strathspey. Arr. by W. B. LAYBOURN.

D.C. *Segue Reel.*

∨ Up Bow. Two Up or Down Bows.
KÖHLERS' "VIOLIN REPOSITORY," 11 NORTH BRIDGE, EDINBURGH.

THE DUNCE DINGS A'.—Reel.

Fine.

FRANCIS SITWELL.—Strathspey. *Arranged by* W. B. LAYBOURN.

Segue Reel. D.C.

CAPTAIN KEELER'S REEL. *Arranged by* W. B. LAYBOURN.

D.C. Fine.

THE NAVVIE ON THE LINE.—Hornpipe.

By Jas. Hill.
Arranged by W. B. Laybourn.

MORPETH RANT.

SPANISH DOLLAR.—Hornpipe.

Arranged by W. B. Laybourn.

(To be continued.)

∨ Up Bow.

Köhlers' "Violin Repository," 11 North Bridge, Edinburgh.

KÖHLERS' VIOLIN REPOSITORY.

No 7.]   PRICE 4D.   [COPYRIGHT.

NAPOLEON'S CORONATION MARCH. *Arranged by* W. B. LAYBOURN.

V Up Bow.   ⊓ Down Bow.   ‑·‑·‑ Two Up or Down Bows.

KÖHLERS' "VIOLIN REPOSITORY," 11 NORTH BRIDGE, EDINBURGH.

50

∨ Up Bow.　　　⊓ Down Bow.　　　•——• Two Up or Down Bows.
KÖHLERS' "VIOLIN REPOSITORY," 11 NORTH BRIDGE, EDINBURGH.

LORD ROTHES' STRATHSPEY.

Composed by Alex. Deas.

D.C.

Segue Reel.

LADY ROTHES' REEL.

Composed by Alex. Deas.

Fine.

JIG.

Composed by Alex. Deas.

| 1st time. | 2nd time. |

** The above Strathspey and Reel are sometimes played in D.

∨ Up Bow. ⊓ Down Bow. ━━━ Two Up or Down Bows.

Köhlers' "Violin Repository," 11 North Bridge, Edinburgh.

KEMP'S HORNPIPE.

Arranged by W. B. LAYBOURN.

THE PEAR TREE.

By JAMES HILL.
Arranged by W. B. LAYBOURN.

CRAZY JANE.—Reel.

Arranged by W. B. LAYBOURN.

D.C.

∨ Up Bow.   ⊓ Down Bow.
KÖHLERS' "VIOLIN REPOSITORY," 11 NORTH BRIDGE, EDINBURGH.

JOHNNY MILLICENT'S HORNPIPE.   *Arr. by* W. B. Laybourn.

HORNPIPE.   *Arranged by* W. B. Laybourn.

HASLAM'S HORNPIPE.   *Arr. by* W. B. Laybourn.

54

HIGHLAND FLING. *Arranged by* W. B. LAYBOURN.

D.C.

Segue Reel.

ROB ROY'S REEL. *Arranged by* W. B. LAYBOURN.

Fine.

STUMPIE STRATHSPEY. *Arranged by* W. B. LAYBOURN.

Segue Reel.

∨ Up Bow. ⊓ Down Bow.

KÖHLERS' "VIOLIN REPOSITORY," 11 NORTH BRIDGE, EDINBURGH.

THE DEIL AMONG THE TAILORS.—Reel.

Arranged by W. B. LAYBOURN.

Fine.

LADY MARY RAMSEY STRATHSPEY.

Arranged by W. B. LAYBOURN.

Segue Reel.

FAIRY DANCE.

Arranged by W. B. LAYBOURN.

D.C.

Fine.

∨ Up Bow.   ⊓ Down Bow.

KÜHLERS' "VIOLIN REPOSITORY," 11 NORTH BRIDGE, EDINBURGH.

MISS GAYTON'S DANCE. *Arranged by* W. B. LAYBOURN.

THE STEAMBOAT HORNPIPE. *Arranged by* W. B. LAYBOURN.

BLACKSMITH'S HORNPIPE. *Arranged by* W. B. LAYBOURN.

(To be continued.)
∨ Up Bow.

KÖHLERS' "VIOLIN REPOSITORY," 11 NORTH BRIDGE, EDINBURGH.

KÖHLERS' VIOLIN REPOSITORY.

No 8.]   PRICE 4D.   [COPYRIGHT.

JOHNNY COPE—Variations. *Arranged by* W. B. LAYBOURN.

Fine.

58

Selection of IRISH REELS.

Arr. by W. B. LAYBOURN.

KEEP IT UP.—Reel.

D.C.

IRISH REEL.

D.C.

OLD IRELAND.—Reel. *Composed by* W. B. LAYBOURN, 1881.

D.C.

v Up Bow. ⊓ Down Bow.

KÖHLERS' "VIOLIN REPOSITORY," 11 NORTH BRIDGE, EDINBURGH

59

THE DEAN BRIDGE, EDINBRO'. *Composed by the* REV. MR. TOUGH.
Six Strathspeys and Reels arranged by W. B. LAYBOURN.

Segue Reel.

I'LL KISS THE BONNIE LASS.—Reel.

D.C. Fine.

THE MARCHIONESS OF HUNTLEY'S STRATHSPEY. *By* MARSHALL.

D.C. Segue Reel.

∨ Up Bow. ⊓ Down Bow. ⁓ Two Up or Down Bows.

KÖHLERS' "VIOLIN REPOSITORY," 11 NORTH BRIDGE, EDINBURGH.

LADY GEORGINA RUSSELL'S REEL.

By Marshall.

D.C. Fine.

KINRARA STRATHSPEY.

By Marshall.

Segue Reel. D.C.

THE MARQUIS OF BOWMONT'S REEL.

By Marshall.

D.C. Fine.

∨ Up Bow. ⊓ Down Bow. Two Up or Down Bows.

Köhlers' "Violin Repository," 11 North Bridge, Edinburgh.

PRINCE ALFRED'S HORNPIPE.

Composed by W. B. LAYBOURN.

EDINBRO' NORTH BRIDGE HORNPIPE.

Composed by W. B. LAYBOURN.

BISHOP AUCKLAND FLOWER SHOW HORNPIPE.

Composed by W. B. LAYBOURN, 1857.

∨ Up Bow.   ⊓ Down Bow.

PRINCE OF WALES' HORNPIPE.
Composed by W. B. LAYBOURN.

NICOLSON STREET HORNPIPE.
Composed by W. B. LAYBOURN.

STAR HORNPIPE.
Composed by W. B. LAYBOURN.

∨ Up Bow. ⊓ Down Bow.

KÖHLERS' "VIOLIN REPOSITORY," 11 NORTH BRIDGE, EDINBURGH.

Selection—OLD TOWLER. *Arranged by* W. B. LAYBOURN.

THE NUT.—Contre Dance.

THE EAST NEUK OF FIFE—Variations.

(To be continued.)

v Up Bow.   ⊓ Down Bow.

Köhlers' "Violin Repository," 11 North Bridge, Edinburgh.

KÖHLERS' VIOLIN REPOSITORY.

No 9.]   PRICE 4D.   [COPYRIGHT.

EAST NEUK OF FIFE—Continued.   *Arranged by* W. B. LAYBOURN.

2nd time, 8va. 3rd position.

Fine.

ᴠ Up Bow.

66

BLAYDEN FLATS.—Hornpipe. *Arranged by* W. B. LAYBOURN.

JENKINS' HORNPIPE. *Arranged by* W. B. LAYBOURN.

HORNPIPE. *Arranged by* W. B. LAYBOURN.

∨ Up Bow.　⊓ Down Bow.
KÖHLERS' "VIOLIN REPOSITORY," 11 NORTH BRIDGE, EDINBURGH.

67

THE FANCY.

Composed by W. B. LAYBOURN.

BURNS'S HORNPIPE.

Arranged by W. B. LAYBOURN.

JACKY TAR.

Arranged by W. B. LAYBOURN.

∨ Up Bow. ⊓ Down Bow. ·‒·‒ Two Up or Down Bows.

1. **THE SOUTH OF THE GRAMPIANS.—Strathspey.**

Six Strathspeys and Reels arranged by W. B. LAYBOURN.

Segue Reel.

2.

Fine.

3. **THE DUCHESS OF ATHOLE'S STRATHSPEY.**

Segue Reel.

∨ Up Bow. ⊓ Down Bow. ⌐••⌐ Two Up or Down Bows.

Köhlers' "Violin Repository," 11 North Bridge, Edinburgh.

4. **THE WIND THAT SHAKES THE BARLEY.—Reel.**

Arranged by W. B. LAYBOURN.

Fine.

5. **MR. MORAY OF ABERCARNEY'S STRATHSPEY.**

Arranged by W. B. LAYBOURN.

D.C.

Segue Reel.

6. **THE COUNTESS OF SUTHERLAND'S REEL.** *By* GEN. JENKINS.

Fine.

ᐯ Up Bow. ⊓ Down Bow.

KÖHLERS' "VIOLIN REPOSITORY," 11 NORTH BRIDGE, EDINBURGH.

CALEDONIAN QUADRILLES.

Arranged by W. B. LAYBOURN.

V Up Bow. ⊓ Down Bow. ⌐⌐ Two Up or Down Bows.

KÖHLERS' "VIOLIN REPOSITORY," 11 NORTH BRIDGE, EDINBURGH.

4.

5.

Fine. D.C.

THE CLOG STOP DANCE.

D.C.

∨ Up Bow.   ⊓ Down Bow.   ⌐·⌐ Two Up or Down Bows.

Köhlers' "Violin Repository," 11 North Bridge, Edinburgh.

M'DONALD'S FANCY.—Strathspey.

Six Strathspeys and Reels arranged by W. B. LAYBOURN.

Segue Reel.

LORD M'DONALD'S REEL.

Fine.

STRATHSPEY.

(To be continued.) *Segue Reel. D.C.*

V Up Bow. ⊓ Down Bow. Two Up or Down Bows.

KÜHLERS' "VIOLIN REPOSITORY," 11 NORTH BRIDGE, EDINBURGH.

KÖHLERS' VIOLIN REPOSITORY.

No 10.]   PRICE 4D.   [COPYRIGHT.

4.

JENNY'S BAWBEE—Reel.
Fingered and Bow Marks by W. B. LAYBOURN.

D.C.

Fine.

5.

THE NORTH BRIDGE—Strathspey.

Segue Reel.

6.

SLEEPY MAGGIE—Reel.

Fine.

∨ Up Bow.   ⊓ Down Bow.

KÖHLERS' "VIOLIN REPOSITORY," 11 NORTH BRIDGE, EDINBURGH.

THE "ANNIE" SCHOTTISCHE.

By WILCOX.

D.C.

LOVE VALSE.

v Up Bow. ⊓ Down Bow. •—•— Two Up or Down Bows.

Kühlers' "Violin Repository," 11 North Bridge, Edinburgh.

FURIOSO GALLOP.

THE ROSE POLKA.

Composed by W. B. LAYBOURN.

∨ Up Bow. ⊓ Down Bow. •–•– Two Up or Down Bows.

Köhlers' "Violin Repository," 11 North Bridge, Edinburgh.

1.
KENO REEL.
Six American Reels and Hornpipes.

D.C.

2.
ANYBODY'S HORNPIPE.

3.
SCITUATE REEL.

∨ Up Bow.   ⊓ Down Bow.

KÖHLERS' "VIOLIN REPOSITORY," 11 NORTH BRIDGE, EDINBURGH.

4. EIGHT BELLS—Hornpipe.

5. SAIL IN, BOYS—Hornpipe.

6. BOB CHADDUCK'S JIG.

V Up Bow.   ⊓ Down Bow.
Köhlers' "Violin Repository," 11 North Bridge, Edinburgh.

78

CRAIGELLACHIE BRIDGE—Strathspey.

Arranged by W. B. LAYBOURN.

D.C.

Segue Reel.

MISS JANE M'INNES'S REEL.

MARSHALL.

D.C.

Fine.

∨ Up Bow.　⊓ Down Bow.　Two Up or Down Bows.
KÖHLERS' "VIOLIN REPOSITORY," 11 NORTH BRIDGE, EDINBURGH.

MISS GRACE MENZIES' STRATHSPEY.
MARSHALL.

D.C.

Segue Reel.

MRS. CHARLES STEWART'S REEL.
MARSHALL.

Fine.

THE CRAIGELLACHIE LASSES—Jig.
MARSHALL.

D.C.

∨ Up Bow.   ⊓ Down Bow.   _._ Two Up or Down Bows.
KÖHLERS' "VIOLIN REPOSITORY," 11 NORTH BRIDGE, EDINBURGH.

CHAMBERS'S HORNPIPE.

R. STEPHENSON.

THE FIDDLER'S CRAMP—Hornpipe.

SHAW'S TRIP TO LONDON—Hornpipe.

T. SHAW.

(To be continued.)

∨ Up Bow.

KÜHLERS' "VIOLIN REPOSITORY," 11 NORTH BRIDGE, EDINBURGH.

KÖHLERS' VIOLIN REPOSITORY.

No 11.]   PRICE 4D.   [COPYRIGHT.

SYLVANUS HORNPIPE.
Bowing and Fingering arranged by W. B. LAYBOURN.

3rd Position.

FLOWERS OF EDINBRO'.

FIREFLY HORNPIPE.

∨ Up Bow.

KÖHLERS' "VIOLIN REPOSITORY," 11 NORTH BRIDGE, EDINBURGH.

NEWMARKET HORSE-RACE; OR, JOHN PATERSON'S MARE GOES FOREMOST.

∨ Up Bow. ⌐—•—• Two Up or Down Bows.
KÖHLERS' "VIOLIN REPOSITORY," 11 NORTH BRIDGE, EDINBURGH.

NEWCASTLE SCHOTTISCHE.

1st time. | 2nd time. D.C.

CALTON VALSE.

By J. Hamilton.

1st time. | 2nd time.

D.C.

V Up Bow. ⊓ Down Bow. Two Up or Down Bows.
Köhlers' "Violin Repository," 11 North Bridge, Edinburgh.

THE ROYAL RECOVERY STRATHSPEY.

D.C.

Segue Reel.

O'SHEA'S COMICAL REEL.

D.C.

Fine.

INVERARAY CASTLE.

FRASER.

Segue Reel. D.C.

∨ Up Bow.　⊓ Down Bow.　⎯⎯ Two Up or Down Bows.

Köhlers' "Violin Repository," 11 North Bridge, Edinburgh.

THE DRAM SHELL.—Reel. FRASER.

D.C.
Fine.

LAYBOURN M'DONALD'S STRATHSPEY. *Composed by* LAYBOURN.

Segue Reel.

LAYBOURN M'DONALD'S REEL. *Composed by* W. B. LAYBOURN.

Fine.

TRIP TO DUBLIN—Jig.

JESSIE THE FLOW'R OF DUNBLANE—Hornpipe.

C. ROCK.

CLOG HORNPIPE.

PRINCE ALBERT'S HORNPIPE.

J. HILL.

∨ Up Bow.

KÖHLERS' "VIOLIN REPOSITORY," 11 NORTH BRIDGE, EDINBURGH.

THE CAGE HORNPIPE.

JAMES HILL.

THE RINK HORNPIPE.

Composed by W. B. LAYBOURN.

GIPSY'S HORNPIPE.

∨ Up Bow. ⊓ Down Bow.

KÖHLERS' "VIOLIN REPOSITORY," 11 NORTH BRIDGE, EDINBURGH.

88

GILLIE CALLUM STRATHSPEY—Sword Dance.

MR. THOS. JARVIS'S REEL.

WHISTLE OWRE THE LAVE O'T.

(To be continued.)

V Up Bow. ⊓ Down Bow. Two Up or Down Bows.

KÖHLERS' "VIOLIN REPOSITORY," 11 NORTH BRIDGE, EDINBURGH.

KÖHLERS' VIOLIN REPOSITORY.

No 12.]   PRICE 4D.   [COPYRIGHT.

GEM SCHOTTISCHE.
Bowing and Fingering arranged by W. B. LAYBOURN.

SWEETHEART SCHOTTISCHE.

DUTCH POLKA.

∨ Up Bow.   ⊓ Down Bow.   •‿• Two Up or Down Bows.
KÖHLERS' "VIOLIN REPOSITORY," 11 NORTH BRIDGE, EDINBURGH.

THE MARQUIS OF HUNTLY—Strathspey. (Variations).

D.C.

Segue Reel.

COLONEL M'BAIN'S REEL.

Fine.

∨ Up Bow.   ∏ Down Bow.   ⎯⎯ Two Up or Down Bows.

KÖHLERS' "VIOLIN REPOSITORY," 11 NORTH BRIDGE, EDINBURGH.

THE HIGHLANDS OF BANFFSHIRE—Strathspey. FRASER.

D.C.
Segue Reel.

CAMERONIAN RANT.

Fine.

Fine. D.C.

MRS. GARDEN OF TROUP—Strathspey.

1st time. | 2nd time.

Segue Reel.

ᐯ Up Bow.   ᐟ—ᐟ Two Up or Down Bows.
KÖHLERS' "VIOLIN REPOSITORY," 11 NORTH BRIDGE, EDINBURGH.

LADY WALLACE—Reel.

Fine.

GENERAL GARIBALDI—Strathspey. *By* J. F. FETTES, D.M.

Segue Reel.

GENERAL GARIBALDI—Reel. *By* J. F. FETTES, D.M.

Fine.

P. BAILLIE'S STRATHSPEY.

By P. BAILLIE.

Segue Reel.

RACHEL RAE—Reel.

MR. LOWE.

Fine.

SWARD HOUSE—Jig.

ᵛ Up Bow.   ⌣⌣ Two Up or Down Bows.

KÖHLERS' "VIOLIN REPOSITORY," 11 NORTH BRIDGE, EDINBURGH.

RUBY—Hornpipe.

MARCELIA—Hornpipe.

UNDERHAND HORNPIPE.

JAMES HILL.

∨ Up Bow.   ⊓ Down Bow.

KÖHLERS' "VIOLIN REPOSITORY," 11 NORTH BRIDGE, EDINBURGH.

STEPHENSON'S HORNPIPE.

R. STEPHENSON, Newcastle.

GIPSY'S· HORNPIPE.

GLEN'S HORNPIPE.

∨ Up Bow. ⊓ Down Bow.

KÖHLERS' "VIOLIN REPOSITORY," 11 NORTH BRIDGE, EDINBURGH.

THE HON. MISS DRUMMOND OF PERTH—Strathspey.

D.C.

Segue Reel.

MISS JOHNSTON'S REEL.

Fine.

BOB AT THE BOWSTER.

1st time.

D.C.

2nd time.

(To be continued.)

∨ Up Bow.　⊓ Down Bow.　‾‿‾ Two Up or Down Bows.

KÖHLERS' "VIOLIN REPOSITORY," 11 NORTH BRIDGE, EDINBURGH.

MUSICAL TREASURY.

Published by ERNEST KÖHLER & SON, II North Bridge, Edinburgh.

YEARLY, Post Free, 2s. 6d.

1885.

OCTOBER.—No. 77.   SECULAR.   MONTHLY, Price 2d.

INVENTIONS EXHIBITION,
CENTRAL GALLERY, WEST-END STALL, No. 3,847.
A Variety of Letter-Note Publications and Appliances on View.

IMPORTANT TO ALL TEACHERS OF SINGING!!

The Simplest and Easiest Method of learning to Sing at Sight from the Staff, is by means of the LETTER-NOTE SYSTEM combining the advantages of the TONIC SOL-FA with the acknowledged Superiority of the OLD NOTATION.

Key E. Round for 4 voices.

Health, hap - pi - ness, plea - sure, Peace, joy with-out mea - sure,

Good for-tune and trea - sure,— All be thine!

EDUCATIONAL WORKS FOR PRIVATE SCHOOLS, CHOIRS, AND EVENING CLASSES.

ELEMENTARY SINGING MASTER, by David Colville. A Complete Course of Instruction on the Method. 80 pp., cloth, 1s. 6d.; paper, 1s. In this course the notes are gradually withdrawn, training the pupils to dispense with their aid.

ELEMENTARY SINGING SCHOOL. Being the Exercises in the above work, published separately, for use of pupils, in 2 parts. 3d. each, in wrapper.

A GRADUATED COURSE of Elementary Instruction in Singing, by David Colville and George Bentley. In this course the Sol-fa initials are gradually withdrawn. In cloth, 1s. 6d.; in wrapper, 1s.

THE PUPIL'S HANDBOOK, containing the Songs, Exercises, &c., in the above course, published separately. In 2 parts, 3d. each.

In the following Courses the Notes are Lettered throughout:—

LETTER-NOTE SINGING METHOD. A course of Elementary Instruction in Singing arranged principally in Four-Part Harmony. Cloth, 1s. 6d.; paper, 1s.

CHORAL GUIDE. Being the Exercises of the above work, published separately in 2 parts, price 3d. each, in wrapper. This is a systematic elementary course, leading the Student by easy stages to a conversance with the art of sight-singing.

THE CHORAL PRIMER. A Course of Elementary Training, by David Colville. 48 pp. in wrapper, price 6d.; or in six 8-page Nos., 1d. each; contains a more thorough and complete course of training than any other work published at the price.

SCHOOL MUSIC. Revised and enlarged edition. Part I., 32 pp., stitched in paper cover, price 3d., containing a complete course for Junior Pupils, with the addition of Voice-training Exercises and Elementary Instruction in the Theory of Music. This is without exception the cheapest and most systematic educational work ever published.

THE JUNIOR COURSE. A Course of Elementary Practice in Singing. by David Colville. Arranged for two trebles, with ad lib. bass. In 6 penny numbers.

LETTER-NOTE VOCALIST. For Class and Home Singing, being a carefully chosen selection of favourite high class Melodies, arranged as Duets and Trios; 4 pages full music size; price, stitched in paper cover, 3d. each. Twelve Numbers already published.

Just Published.

THE INTERMEDIATE SIGHT-SINGER, a thorough and systematic work of intermediate instruction in music, leading the student by easy stages to a thorough conversance with the art of sight-singing. The music is in four-part harmony and short score, forming an accompaniment if required, but is so arranged that it can be sung in two parts by omitting tenor and bass. This arrangement in itself is of great advantage, as it adapts the works for schools as well as Choral Societies and Evening Classes. In two parts of 16 pages, price 3d. each, in wrapper.

EASY CANTATAS, S.A.T.B., with Solos, &c., printed in Letter-Note. Pilgrims of Ocean, 4d.; Maypole, 3d.

LIBERAL TERMS TO PROFESSION, CATALOGUES FREE ON APPLICATION.

For Government, National, and Board Schools.
IMPORTANT TO SCHOOLMASTERS AND OTHERS.

The Letter-Note Method has obtained Government recognition, and Letter-Note pupils are entitled to have the Sol-fa initials appended to the sight-singing test supplied by the School Inspector.

THE CODE SINGER (Letter-Note) for the use of the different divisions in singing under the New Code. Staff Notation—1st Division.—Code Singer, Nos. 1, 2 and 3, price 1d. each. Of these the first two contain the exercises absolutely necessary for the Code requirements, the third being an amplification of the others. The three numbers bound together in wrapper, with extra words for the tunes, price 3d.

2nd Division, Standard I.—Code Singer, Nos. 4, 5, and 6, price 1d. each. Of these Nos. 4 and 5 only are necessary for Code training where economy is desired, No. 6 containing additional songs and exercises. The three numbers bound together in wrapper, with extra words for tunes, price 3d.

3rd Division, Standards II. and III.—Code Singer, Nos. 7, 8, 9, and 10, price 1d. each. The four numbers stitched together in wrapper, price 4d.

4th Division, Standard IV. and upwards—Code Singer, Nos. 11, 12, 13, and 14, price 1d. each. The four numbers stitched together in wrapper, price 4d.

CODE SINGER—TEACHERS' EDITION. Containing the Code Examination Tests, with conditions and directions as to Examination by H.M. Inspector; also Educational Processes, Model Pointing and Ear Exercises, and Hints on Teaching.

Divisions I. and II., Teachers' Edition, including Code Singer, Nos. 1 to 6, in all 64 pages, price 5d., now ready.

Divisions III. and IV., Teachers' Edition, including Code Singer, Nos. 7 to 14, 80 pages, price 10d., in press.

LONDON: J. ADLEY & CO., Letter-Note Publishers, 26 Cornwall Road, Finsbury Park, N.; F. PITMAN, 20 Paternoster Row, E.C.
EDINBURGH: E. KÖHLER & SON, 11 North Bridge; JOHN MENZIES & CO., 12 Hanover St.
GLASGOW: JOHN MENZIES & CO., 21 Drury Street; MORISON BROTHERS, Buchanan Street.

A LESSON IN LOVE.

A TALE.

"WHAT is the matter, little woman?"

"Only tired, John."

Lina Reynolds looked up as she spoke, to smile bravely into the face bending anxiously over her.

"Tired, Lina?" he said, lifting the little figure as he spoke, and taking his wife like a child upon his knee. "What have you been doing to tire you?"

"Only the day's work. Don't worry, John," for a shade passed over the kindly face.

"I don't worry; but I can't see what makes you complain so often of being tired. I am sure the housework ain't so much. Other women do it!"

There was just a little fretfulness in John's tone, though he did not mean to be unkind.

"I know they do. Mrs. Harper has four children, and takes care of them in addition to housework, besides doing piles of sewing. Perhaps, John, it is because I have not had experience in country work, and don't manage well. I will learn better after awhile. Now, tell me what you did in town."

"I did quite well. Sold the whole crop of wheat at a good price, and put another instalment in the bank for the Stanley farm."

"Your heart is set on that farm, John."

"Indeed it is! Let me once own that clear of debt, and I shall be a happy man. It is the best land in the country, and the house is twice as large as this!"

Lina thought of larger floors to scrub, more rooms to clean, and additional work of all kinds, and swallowed a little sigh that nearly escaped her.

"John," she said, rather timidly, "don't you think if you spent part of the money on this house we might be very happy here?"

"Spend money on this house?" cried the astonished John. "Why, what on earth ails this house?"

"I mean in things for it. Now, the parlour looks so stiff, and is always shut up. I was thinking if we had a pretty carpet and some curtains of white muslin or lace, and a set of nice furniture, and—and—a piano. Oh, John, if I could have a nice piano."

John Reynolds looked at his wife as if she had proposed to him to buy up the crown jewels of Russia.

"A piano! Do you know what a piano costs?"

"No. Aunt Louise had one, you know, over since I can remember. But I think if we had a pretty parlour to rest in, in the evening, I could play for you and sing. You never heard me play and sing, John?"

"I have heard you sing, but not lately," said John, rather gloomily.

"Oh! that was just humming around the house. I mean real singing. I have lots of music in my trunk."

"But you are only a farmer's wife now, Lina. I thought you understood when we were married that you were not to have any city finery or pleasure."

"So I did, John. I don't want any finery. I don't want any pleasure but your love, John. Don't scowl up you face so. I am silly to think of these things at all. There, kiss me and forget it. I am nicely rested now, and I will get your tea in ten minutes."

John put her down with a very tender kiss, and straightway fell into a reverie.

Lina Rivers had been a district school teacher in Scottfield just four months, when John Reynolds offered her his hand and heart. She was an orphan from infancy, but her father's sister had adopted and educated her in a life of luxury, and died without altering a will made years before, leaving her entire fortune to a charity asylum. Lina, left alone, had thankfully accepted the position of county school teacher, procured for her by her friends, and was thinking life a hard burden, when John came to brighten it. She gave her whole gentle little heart into his keeping at once, appreciating at their full value his honest, true heart, his frank nature, his sterling good qualities, and looking with the most profound admiration upon his tall, strong frame and handsome face.

It was a perfect love match, for John fairly worshipped the dainty, refined little beauty he had married. And, having married her, he took her to his home, and, in all ignorance, proceeded to kill her.

There was no blame to be laid upon him. Living in the old farm-house where he had spent his entire life, the one ambition of his heart was to own land, stock, barns, and a model farm.

He had seen his mother cook, churn, feed poultry, and drudge all her life; all the women he knew did the same; and if Lina made odd mistakes she put a willing heart into her work and soon conquered its difficulties. Surely, he thought, it was an easier life to be mistress of his home, with the Stanley farm in prospect, than to toil over stupid children in a district school. He had never seen velvet carpets and lace curtains, grand pianos, dainty silks, and other surroundings that were Lina's from babyhood. He had never heard the wonderful music the little white hands, all rough and scarred now, could draw from the ivory keys of an organ or piano, or the clear, pure voice in song. It was an unknown world to John where his wife's memory lingered as she scoured tins, strained milk, and cooked huge dishes of food for the farm hands. He would have thought it wicked waste, if not positive insanity, to draw from the bank his hard-earned savings to invest them in beautifying his plain, comfortable home.

And Lina lashed her conscience sharply, telling herself she was ungrateful, repining, and wicked. Was not John tender, true, and loving? Where among her city friends was there a heart like his? Had she not known he was only a farmer?

And so the loving little woman toiled and slaved, undertook tasks far beyond her strength, worked early and late, until, just one year after his wedding day, John Reynolds, coming home to his tea, found lying upon the kitchen floor a little, senseless figure, with a face like death, and hands that sent a chill to his very heart.

The doctor, hastily summoned, looked grave, and advised perfect quiet and rest. A girl was hired, and John tenderly nursed the invalid, but, though she grew better, she was still pale and weak.

"Take her away awhile," said the doctor. "Try change of air. She is overworked."

"But," said honest, puzzled John, "she does nothing but the housework for us two. She has no child, and our sewing is not much."

The doctor looked into the troubled face. "You are a good man, John Reynolds, and a strong one," he said; "will you let me tell you a few truths?"

"Yes. About Lina?"

"About Lina. You remember, do you not, the tiny antelope you admired so much in the menagerie we had here last summer?"

"Certainly," said John, looking more puzzled than ever.

"Suppose you had bought that little creature, and yoked it with one of your oxen to a cart to do the same work?"

"I'd been a fool," cried John, "that little thing couldn't work. It is just made pretty to look at and play with,"

"That's it, John. Now, I don't think God ever made a woman to look pretty and play, but he made some for the rough work of the world and some for the dainty places, some to cook and scrub, and some to draw men's souls to heaven by gentle loveliness. Your wife is one of the latter. If you were a poor man I would have held my tongue, but you are a rich one. Give your wife a servant, let her have books, music, pretty things around her. Let her rest from toil, and you may keep her by your side; put her back in her old place and you may order her tombstone, for she will soon need it. Don't put your antelope beside your oxen, John."

"I will not! Thank you! I understand. Poor, loving, patient heart!"

"That's right. Take her now for a little pleasure trip, and get back her roses."

Lina clapped her hands when John asked her if she would like to spend a week in New York, and really seemed to draw a new life from the very idea.

It was delicious fun to see John's wide-open eyes as they entered the parlour of the great city hotel and were shown into the bed-room, whose beauties were quite as bewildering.

"The best room," he told the landlord, and Lina could not repress a cry of delight, at the vista of a cosy sitting-room with a piano standing invitingly open.

"O, John!" she said, "won't you go in there and shut the door for five minutes, please?"

John obeyed, of course. John, she thought gratefully, refused her nothing now.

"How lucky I brought some of my old dresses!" Lina thought. "I have not worn them since I was a school-marm. Fancy Mrs. Reynolds scrubbing the floor in this dress!"

John rubbed his eyes and pinched himself as a figure sailed in the sitting-room, made him a sweeping courtesy, and went to the piano.

Was that the little woman who had worn prints and sun-bonnets so long? The fair hair was fashionably dressed, and hands of blue velvet looped the golden curls. A dress of blue silk, with softest lace trimmings and ornaments of pearls, had certainly made a fine lady of Lina. The piano was yielding its most bewitching tones to the skilled little fingers, and John's bewilderment was complete when a voice of exquisite sweetness, though not powerful, began to sing.

Only one song, full of thrills and quavers, and then Lina rushed from the piano into John's arms.

"John, darling," she said, "hold me fast. Don't let me slip from you!"

"O, Lina!" he groaned, "I was not fit to marry such a dainty bird! But I loved you, little one."

"And I love you, John; rough old John. Let me sing again. I am very happy to-day, my husband."

But the wonderful thrills filled the little room now. In a clear, pure voice, full of expression, Lina sang—

"I know that my Redeemer liveth."

Every word fell like hot tears on poor John's heart; until, as the last chord trembled upon the air, Lina turned to him, stretching out her arms.

"Take me in your arms, John!"

He took her tenderly to the room she had quitted so gaily, and replaced her finery by a white wrapper whose lace trimmings looked like fairy work to his unaccustomed eyes.

"Are you tired, love?" he asked, with a great spasm of terror at his heart, as he looked at the white, wasted face.

"Yes, very, very tired, but happy, John!" and with a little sigh of entire content, Lina nestled down against the warm heart whose every throb she knew was all her own. The white lids fell softly over the violet eyes, and she slept peacefully as a child.

Softly as she rested, the faint pink flush gathered on her fair cheek and a smile crept over her lips, while John, bending over her, lifted his heart in earnest prayer for the life that made his own so bright.

Mrs. Reynolds was to experience her share of astonishment during her holiday, and it commenced by the apparition of John the next day in a suit of handsome clothes that well became his manly figure. There was no foppery, but he looked a gentleman, though he made more than one grimace before he got, as he said, "well shaken into store clothes."

Can I describe that week? What was new to John was old familiar ground to Lina. Central Park was not soon exhausted, and the little guide grew stronger and rosier every day in John's thoughtful care, that provided plenty of pleasant excitement, but guarded against fatigue.

It was early in the afternoon of a sunny day, when the train drew up at Scottfield station, and John handed his wondering wife into a neat little one-horse carriage waiting for them.

"A new purchase, dear!" he explained. "We are to have a drive every afternoon. Dr. Greyson prescribed it."

The house was where it had always been, but Lina rubbed her eyes and wondered if she had been suddenly carried into fairy-land.

The dull little sitting-room had been papered, carpeted, curtained, and transformed into a cosy dining-room. The stiff parlour was a very bower of beauty, with a fine piano, the daintiest of furniture, soft muslin curtains, and a carpet covered with boquets of exquisite flowers; the bed-rooms were carpeted brightly, and rejoiced in cottage sets, and in the kitchen the most good-natured of stout German girls fairly shed tears when Lina addressed her in her own language.

"But, John!" she cried, "the Stanley farm?"

"Is sold, dear. You were right; we will make this home so lovely the Stanley farm will never cost me a sigh. Dr. Greyson and his wife took all the trouble here, and I have hired two new hands, so as to have a little more leisure."

"But, John," the little wife said earnestly, "I do not want you to think me a fine lady—a doll to wear fine clothes and live in idleness. I want to be truly a helpmate to you."

"So you will be, Lina. God meant no one to be a drone in the busy hive of the world. You are not strong, but you will find plenty to keep you busy in superintending indoor arrangements and directing Gretchen. And in our drives, love, we will see if we cannot find some poorer than ourselves to comfort and aid. That will be my thank-offering for your life, my little wife."

The neighbours stared and wondered. Comments upon John's folly and improvidence fell from many lips, and old men, shaking their heads, prophesied ruin for the Reynolds farm.

But John was as much astonished as any of them, when, after a few years, he found the farm yielding him a larger income than ever before.

"I do believe, Lina," he said one day, to a matronly little woman, who was dressing a crowing baby, "that your flower garden last year was worth a hundred pounds to me."

"John!"

"You see it was to get you the information about flowers that we first began to subscribe to *The Agriculturist*: there I found so many hints that I began to think I knew nothing about farming. One book after another crept into the house, and the time I thought would be wasted, taken from farm-work, was spent in reading. Now, look at the labour-saving machines I have bought! See the new stock! My orchard is going to be the best in the country, too."

"And my poultry-yard, John! it was the papers and magazines that first gave me the idea of a model poultry-yard. What fun we had, John, getting it started!"

"Yes, indeed. That New York trip was the best investment I ever made, Lina. I saw so many things there that I recognised as old friends when I met them again in print—the threshing machine, the rotary harrow, the improved plough."

"And," said Mrs. Reynolds, mischievously, "the Milton watch, the sewing machine, the corals for Johnnie!"

"Come, are you ready for your drive?"

"As soon as I put on my hat and get the basket of things for Mrs. Goodwin."

"It beats me, John," said his uncle, one bright day, "where you find so much money for tomfoolery, new-fangled nonsense, and fallals for Lina, and yet give so much in charity. I thought you were crazy to buy the Stanley farm."

"I was once, but I have something better now than the Stanley farm. I have learned how to manage my antelope."

"What?" But to this day John has never explained that riddle to his puzzled relative.

PROMENADE CONCERTS.

THE indoor or outdoor promenade concert, which is growing in favour with the populace, has cost a great many tears and some wrath to the "genuine musician." The whole-souled man who gets up at five to write a concerto, or to practise for a private quartette, and who sits up till twelve writing his impressions of the last masterpiece of the last musical phenomenon, is apt to be rather sarcastic when the promenade concert is mentioned. It has the dreadful taint of popularity about it, the "hoi polloi" seem to enjoy it, and for that reason, if that alone, it is out of the category of music proper. To his mind there is somewhat of desecration in playing real music to promenaders. Auditors may sit, or they may stand. Sitting is best, for then the eyes can be more conveniently closed, all the muscles relaxed, and the bodily frame brought into a highly receptive state, and become an unobstructed channel for the passage of the current from the musical batteries in the orchestra to the musical Swan-lights in the brain. Standing is allowable where a chair is not to be had, and is, indeed, more respectful in the case of certain classes of music. But to walk about is a kind of profanation, which causes him sore distress. Therefore it is that he has noted with dismay the increasing support given to "go-as-you-please" concerts, for he does not exactly know where it will land the country. It is meet that we should look a little into this matter, and find out, if possible, the *raison d'etre* of the promenade concert. There is a soul of good in most things evil, we are told, and perhaps we may discover even in this phenomenon a little utility. In the first place, we find that the promenade concert is at once an assertion and a recognition of the great English principle of the liberty of the subject. When you have had enough music you can go away, without making yourself an object of observation or disturbing anybody. At the promenade concert you can fish out the morceaux you would like to listen to, and you can lounge through the rest. We should not object to see the principle extended. It would be very nice if, at the theatre, we might walk out when the sorrowful heroine comes on, and have a bell rung in the adjoining smoking-room when it was time for the funny man, or vice versa, according to taste. Then, if we could skip the scientific lecturer's theoretical instruction, and just walk in to his experiments, his explosions, his making a wheel go round very fast, his throwing of coloured lights upon the ladies, and his magnifying a million times the ramifications of a toad's hind leg, it would be very agreeable indeed. We should be very thankful, too, for the same liberty at the public meeting, so that we might hear the movers of resolutions, and cut the seconders and supporters, and leave at any moment when a man began to talk about his reluctance to appear on that occasion, or when we were threatened with "just one word more," or the plate. Then the promenade concert, if it be a hindrance rather than a help to one art, has the merit of promoting another. This may be thought to be rather a negative virtue, but still we must extract what good we can from a thing, though it be not the particular good we seek. Promenade music thaws the frozen tongue. It inspires ideas. It enables people really to enjoy one another's society. To this end, of course, it requires to be pretty loud—as much sound in the music, so much talk among the auditors. A roaring quadrille stirs up the most sluggish imagination, and a blast of a trumpet reminds the dullest of a good anecdote. Amateurs hate anything loud, of course, but we really cannot see any reason in the nature of things why music should not be loud as well as low. The fact is, the more cultured people get, the softer and smaller they like everything: subdued colours in pictures, whispers in oral communication, mere hints in the conveyance of ideas, and (so they say) microscopic helpings of food, till there is a danger of everything being whittled away to nothing. Green grass and blue sky are too glaring, ordinary accents too grating, common language too redundant, and a slice of beef much too sensual, for a great many people already; and if this process is to continue without check, life will become the shadow of a shade. So the promenade concert comes to the rescue in its own province, and vindicates the merits of loudness, fulness, and depth as a correction to culture. There are some incidental advantages of the promenade concert which deserve a note. They benefit only select portions of the community, it is true, but even these should not be slighted. Some people's receptivity is never fully developed when they are sitting or even walking, but only when they are leaning against something. Those who have been brought closely into contact with the British workman, know that he is never so happy as when he is propping up a wall. All through the country you may see miles of him propping up the houses and the street walls, the garden fences and the village pumps. This is not due, as might at first sight appear, to the instinct of self-preservation and the fear that the walls might tumble down, but to the fact that this peculiar posture encourages a state of receptivity of the mind, and when in it the workman can more readily imbibe the latest local and imperial intelligence. No doubt this is the case with many besides the British workman, so that when we see a gentleman at the promenade concert taking a chair up, and leaning with his arms on the back, or trying to screw his shoulder through the wood-work of the orchestra, or leaning back over the balustrade till his face is out of sight, we may conclude that this is a physical condition of receptivity, and that the music only reaches him when it is fulfilled.

CHURCH CHOIR TRAINING.

By WILLIAM DE MANDY SERGISON.

BAD music in large churches is a great national evil. I have visited some with a reputation for performing a fine musical service, and have found organ and choir equally out of tune throughout, and endless mistakes; in fact, very bad. Under such circumstances thousands of persons are being given "stones for bread" without knowing it, they are being accustomed to listen to, enjoy, and even praise, music that is not music, and to take bad for good. So, gradually, popular taste, and the national ear are being vitiated and debased instead of being cultivated and improved. I never hear such a service as this in a large church where there is a wealthy congregation without feeling inexpressibly indignant and grieved.

Quietness and reverence should be the watchword. If it is possible to avoid it, the attention of the congregation should never be distracted. The waving of a hand is unnecessary, except sometimes in an unobtrusive manner for unaccompanied singing. Even with a full orchestral service in church, the beat of the conductor should be quiet with no superfluous flourish.

The choir-trainer organist should have some one under him who can occasionally take the organ at rehearsal, so that he may hear the choir at a distance and personally correct individuals, which can always be done quietly and unostentatiously, without giving pain. The choir should enter into the spirit of every part of the service they have to sing, and should endeavour to feel, and bring out, the meaning of the words by appropriate delivery and hearty earnestness. All eccentricities should be studiously avoided and corrected at rehearsal (the organist indeed must watch himself closely in this respect). Sharpness of attack, crisp clearness should be attained by voices and organ. There should not be (to use Mr. Barnby's expression) any "ragged edges" to be heard.

The accompanist at the organ in church is also the conductor. To be a good one he must have certain qualifications—anticipation, sharpness, idealism, heart, or what is called soul, the power of touching a responsive and sympathetic chord in the hearts of his hearers through his medium, the organ. He must have a power of keeping people together, which should be *felt* both in congregational and in chorus music, so that the hearers should not be in fear, when the music is intricate and difficult, that things must inevitably go to pieces. In this branch of the choirmaster organist's work, the old saying of *Ars est celare artem*, holds good; and, if he is the "secret wire-puller behind the scenes," never unduly obtruding himself, but always ready to help and command, he will fill both choir and congregation with a sense of security and confidence. One very important quality in an accompanist is the conductor's intuitive power of hitting the right time and rhythm of everything he attacks at once at first starting. No good effects can be obtained unless the starts are firm, steady, and decided.

THROAT DISEASES.

EVERY one is familiar with the symptoms of sore throat. These are, the irritation and soreness, the feverish condition, hoarseness, difficulty of swallowing and speaking, &c. Some persons immediately upon entering a room or railway carriage filled with tobacco-smoke experience a tickling and irritation of the throat, producing an irrepressible hacking and coughing, results which are apt to follow the smoking of tobacco; and alcohol, especially when ardent spirits are indulged in, with many persons will produce a well-known and distressing soreness of throat. When predisposition to sore throat and cold prevails, it is a good plan to bathe the surface of the body every morning upon rising. The shower-bath or regular ordinary immersion bath may be employed, or the body may be mopped with a wet towel or sponge, care being taken that the water is *not too cold*.

Great care should be exercised with regard to underclothing when persons are susceptible to the affection under discussion. The undershirt and drawers should be of flannel or of a mixed material in which wool is contained, such as swan's-down, which is far less irritating to the skin. Some persons are extremely intolerant of flannel, which in them produces much irritation. If it can be afforded, silk is the best form of under garment. This article of dress should be of loose texture, and should admit of being easily washed and rendered clean.

The climate of this country being so subject to variations of temperature, it may be advisable to have three kinds of weight of the underclothing—one of somewhat heavy texture for the winter and early spring, a second of medium texture for the spring and autumn, and a third, the lightest texture, to be obtained for the extreme heat of summer; but the heavy fabric should not be changed for the lighter until the change of season is positively present. All underclothing worn during the day should be removed at night, and turned inside out, so as to be thoroughly dried and ventilated before the following morning. The underclothing worn during the day should never be slept in, and that worn at night should never be worn in the day.

It is well for individuals who are specially susceptible to cold to keep the mouth well closed whilst in the open air, and in many cases a respirator will be found useful. With respect to the remedies for sore throat, it may be stated briefly that it is difficult to lay down any hard and fast rules, as the medical attendant will be the best person to consult; but it may be said that warmth is of the greatest importance, and, if it be possible, the sufferer should be kept in a warm room, at a temperature of 70° Fah.

Inhalation of steam is very valuable. This is most conveniently carried out by means of a proper steam inhaler; but if this is not easily available, boiling water may be placed in a suitable vessel and the steam inhaled. Lozenges of tannin, chlorate of potash, tolu, ratany, and others are often used. Astringent gargles may also be employed, of which common alum is perhaps the best.

The term sore throat, in a restricted sense, implies an affection which is limited to a small part of the throat, such as the pharynx, or merely the back of the throat and soft palate, and known by the name of pharyngitis; or it may indicate far more extensive mischief, and embrace a far larger area, extending to the tonsils, and even to the larynx and vocal chords.

Probably in the slightest ordinary cold there is always a certain amount of inflammation of the pharynx present, and this is comparatively of mild significance, but when the deeper structures are involved the case becomes of far more serious character.—*Musical Standard.*

INSTRUMENTAL MUSIC IN CHURCH.

By HENRY MASKELL, BRECON.

THERE still remains in the opinion of many people a doubt as to whether instrumental music should or should not be used in church; and, though this is not always publicly expressed, yet, nevertheless, it is occupied in the minds of many. Even that noble church instrument, the organ, comes in for a share of adverse criticism, it being sometimes looked upon as an intruder (some say an idol) in the house of God, and no allowance is made for the great amount of assistance which the singing receives from the instrument, or how lamentably poor the general effect (in most cases) would be without it. It is, I think, a very little plea (though perhaps laudable in itself) that the voice alone is sufficient in church, and that an instrument is not needed ; but let the holders of this idea consider whether this does not often proceed more from a want of taste for music rather than from any other cause. The voice is certainly of the first importance in the rendering of any kind of music, but in the majority of cases it is in want of a sustaining power—a foundation upon which it can rely. How often the singing would become flat, dry, and unmusical, were it not for the help it receives from the organ ; besides, bright, hearty, well-rendered music is a chief means of attracting good attendances ; and few will deny that our congregations in church might not be made larger. But while the organ is by many allowed to be a necessary and proper means of elevating and improving church music, the introduction of string and other instruments into the service would be looked upon as very objectionable, and probably cause a general exodus among the congregation. Let us see whether this would be right. In looking at the subject from its true point, we find in the Scriptures that many, and perhaps all the then known kinds of instruments were used in the old Jewish Church. David, in the Psalms, urges us to praise God with all kinds of instruments—the sound of the trumpet, psaltery, harp, timbrel, and with the loud-sounding cymbals ; and, as these were to be used as a means of praise to God, where could a more fitting place be found for them to render such service than in His own house ? To say that when Christ came to the world the ancient law departed is certainly true, but this applies to the abolition of the types and shadows of our Saviour's first coming rather than to the alteration of the manner of praise in His temple. Since such is the case, why exclude the use of instrumental music from the church?—why banish those things which in ages gone by were used as means of praise to God? To the reverent worshippers the sound of music, rather than diverting the soul from the service, materially adds to a devotional frame of mind. While on this subject we may notice the objections which some have to the performance of oratorios and other sacred works in church. In my opinion, the people who raise such objections are influenced more by their own narrow-mindedness —not to say ignorance—rather than by a sincere desire to maintain the sacredness and perfect purity of the church. To argue that such works are given for the pleasure and vanity of man is hardly sufficient reason to justify the promoters of such performances in giving serious consideration to the views of the "unco guid," who are happily fast becoming an unimportant minority incapable of doing much harm. It is now universally admitted that the use of instrumental music in church is a right and orthodox medium for the praise of God ; but, while rejoicing that this is so, I would say, let us be careful that we neglect not to worship with our hearts as well as with the feeling of devotion induced by the "heavenly sounds" of sacred melody.

ANTONIN DVORÁK.

ONE of the most prominent of the coming men of music indisputably is Antonin Dvorák. Although not by birth one of our own countrymen, his celebrity is almost entirely British. Until he won his first great success in this country, when about three years ago his "Stabat Mater" came in the light of a revelation to English audiences, he was deemed merely one of the *Dii minores* of modern musical Germany. He was patronised by Brahms and championed by Joachim, but few beyond a certain circle were familiar even with his name. Antonin Dvorák is duly grateful for the position the good taste of British music lovers has enabled him to achieve. He has devoted himself assiduously to the study of our manners and language. All the most important of his forthcoming compositions are written specially for England, and part of each year will henceforth be spent by him in this country.

The career of Antonin Dvorák reads like a volume of romance. His fame is far too recent to warrant the admittance of his name to the pages of our standard biographical dictionaries. The composer is, however, himself by no means averse to referring to the humbleness of his origin. Antonin Dvorák was born in 1841 in the neighbourhood of Mülhausen, or, as it is called in the Bohemian dialect, Nelahozeves, a village with a few hundred inhabitants. His father combined the offices of village slaughterman and rural tavern-keeper. Young Dvorák himself in his early years served as pot-boy at the inn, and assisted his father to slaughter, skin, and dress cattle. By the laws, even the poorest lad in the meanest Bohemian village is compelled to learn music as a part of his primary education. Dvorák was taught at the village school, and roughly learned the rudiments, and to sing and fiddle on the violin. When he could play a little he belonged to the village band, which was wont to strike up the dance for the lads and lasses of the neighbourhood after church was over on Sundays. The dancers contributed a few pence each to the expenses of the band, and these slender earnings were divided among the members. When Dvorák was thirteen he went to work for his uncle at the village of Zlonic, close by Schau. There the village schoolmaster was a somewhat superior musician. Dvorák used to sing in the choir, and his master gave him a few lessons on the organ. Finding him an apt pupil the schoolmaster allowed him to copy music, and even to play old ecclesiastical services from a figured bass, an art which the young musician taught himself. He also had a few piano lessons, and was initiated into the rudiments of counterpoint.

When Dvorák was sixteen he was sent to Prague to study at the College of Organists, then directed by Joseph Pitsch. Antonin Dvorák only spoke the Bohemian dialect, and his first difficulty was to teach himself German. Then he was compelled to live upon the scanty allowance of a little over fifteen shillings per month. The struggles of a young man, even at Prague, to lodge, feed, and clothe himself on about £10 per annum can only be imagined. When Pitsch died he was succeeded by a far kinder master, one Kreyci, and under his guidance young Dvorák first made the acquaintance of the music of Mozart, Mendelssohn, and Beethoven. He says the first real orchestral work he ever heard was when he stole into a rehearsal of Beethoven's choral symphony, under Spohr. In 1860, when Dvorák was nineteen, he became a violinist in a band which played at *cafés* and dancing halls, and his wages were £25 per annum. He earned a little overtime by playing in a sextet in order to amuse the insane in a private lunatic asylum. In 1862 he obtained a post in the band of thirty-six at the new Bohemian Opera House at Prague, under Mayer, and it was about this time that his friend Bendl for the first time lent him the score of the Beethoven septet. In 1871 he left the theatre, in order to try and get a living of at least £50 per annum by teaching.

During this struggle Dvorák was not idle. To shortly after this period (in 1873) belongs the "Patriotic Hymn," announced for the last Worcester Festival, but since given in London. He also wrote an opera, "König and Köhler," avowedly in the style of the "Meistersinger." It was tried by the orchestra, unanimously "protested," and withdrawn.

Dvorák was shortly afterwards appointed organist at Adelbett Church, Prague. He sent in his opera and his symphony in F to the Minister in Vienna, and for these he obtained the enormous Government grant of £40. Flushed with success, Dvorák married, and has since lived a very happy wedded life. A year later he made a second attempt, sending in an opera entitled "Wanda" and his "Stabat Mater." Both were ignominiously rejected. The "Stabat Mater"—which established his fame among a more intelligent community, and has set the musicians of two hemispheres wondering whether we have or not discovered a second Beethoven—was not deemed worthy an encouraging grant of £40 by Austrian bureaucracy. He tried again, and got £50. Eventually he sent in several works, and among them the pianoforte concerto in G minor, first introduced in this country by Mr. Manns at the Crystal Palace in October, 1883. Brahms happened to see it, and he and the renowned Viennese critic, Hanslick, exerted themselves sufficiently to obtain for Dvorák a grant of £60. Besides this, Brahms asked Simrock, of Berlin, to publish some of the Bohemian composer's works, and thus they were brought to the notice of Joachim. Mr. Manns had already introduced some of Dvorák's Slav music at the Crystal Palace. But his very name was almost unknown. Joachim's will is, however, puissant at the popular concerts, and when he recommended the production of Dvorák's Sextet in A, Mr. Chappell at once accepted it. The work, first given Feb. 23, 1880, made a great impression, but it was not until 1883, when the "Stabat Mater" was produced here, that the name of the composer came prominently to the front.

The evening of March 10, 1883, may hereafter be deemed historical. Very few of the small audience had the smallest knowledge of the work, the vocal score of which was placed in the hands of most of them as they entered St. James' Hall. Yet another "Stabat Mater," rejected by the Austrian Minister, was not likely to interest those who attended as a business duty, expecting to chronicle yet another pretentious failure. But a very few minutes after Mr. Barnby had lifted his *báton* served to stifle the small talk, and to concentrate the attention of the audience upon the music now heard. Rarely in our time has such a master work from a totally unexpected source been sprung upon a sceptical public. Dvorák leaped at a bound into fame. The Philharmonic Society, sorely in need of a lion, invited him to come to England. Messrs. Novello's firm, who had published his "Stabat Mater," warmly and generously, according to their wont, looked after his interests. Dvorák came here, conducted at the Philharmonic, and directed a gala performance of his "Stabat Mater" at the Albert Hall. The senior partner of Novellos gave a *fête* in his honour at Norwood, and Dvorák declared he had never before seen such a congregation of beautiful ladies. But his tastes were not amid the garish lights of society. He was at home at Mr. Oscar Beringer's, and vastly preferred his lager beer, his pipe, and his chat with friends. Dvorák returned last autumn to direct his "Stabat Mater" at the Three Choirs Festival, and again this summer to conduct at the Philharmonic his new symphony in D minor, expressly composed for this country.

Hitherto most of the music we have heard from the pen of Dvorák has been that composed in his early years, when the young married man was struggling for an artist's stipend of £40. Now, however, for the first time he comes before us at the greatest of our festivals—that of Birmingham—with a cantata specially written for this country. He has in hand an English oratorio on the subject of "Samson and Delilah," and other works. He thus, having cast in his lot with us, has a special title to be considered as a Coming Man. In the judgment of many, he is one of the sole surviving hopes of continuing the long line of great Continental composers. The star of Brahms is on the wane; Raff and Wagner are dead; Gounod is well stricken in years; Verdi cannot, and Boito will not, write any more. The position of the younger generation of French, German, and Italian writers is overshadowed, both here and abroad, by the advance of the composers of England, from Mackenzie, Villiers Stanford, Goring Thomas, and Cowen downwards. It is to Dvorák that the eyes of Europe turn in expectation of hailing another of the race of really great Continental musicians. There are some who are nervous lest adulation and the process of "academising" should injure that which promises to be a great and original genius. On this point it would be the veriest nonsense to attempt prophecy. The result of the highly important essay at the Birmingham Festival will, to a certain extent, tend to indicate whether high hopes are justified or otherwise.

The success of the Birmingham Festival was indisputably won by Herr Dvorák's cantata, "The Spectre's Bride." Despite a ghoulish libretto, and a puerile English version, distilled from the original Bohemian through a German translation, the swing of Dvorák's music carried all before it. Anything more exciting than the chain of choruses—led by Mr. Santley, descriptive of the terrible march of the spectre and his lady love, and relieved by the duets of the unfortunate couple—has rarely been heard. This work (the first choral composition ever written by Dvorák for an English festival) shows the Bohemian composer at his very strongest. The choral parts are somewhat difficult, but it will doubtless be the privilege of many choral societies in the provinces to overcome them,—*Figaro.*

A GREAT obstacle to any improvement in our English sacred music is the prejudice which many people still retain to what they call a "performance" in Church—ignoring the fact that the clergyman always "performs" not only the sermon but a great deal of the service. They do not object to the vicarious offering of prayer by one man ; but they are shocked by the idea of a fairly representative number of people discharging, in the name of the congregation, a duty for which the others have not taken the trouble to qualify themselves. And the very assistance they will not accept in Church, they delight to have in the concert-room. For, in England, there are thousands of people, destitute of general musical proclivities, who, at least annually, attend "performances" of the "Messiah ;" and do so distinctly as a religious exercise, yielding their sympathies freely to the influence of its sublime strains, and consciously warmed and elevated in spirit by the increased pathos and power with which the music endows the words. How funnily moulded our "principles" are?—*Dr. Hiles, in the "Quarterly Musical Review."*

Musical Treasury.

EDINBURGH, OCTOBER 1, 1885.

ADVERTISEMENTS.

Advertisements will be received at the following rate:—

One page,	. . .	£1	0	0
Half page,	. .	0	11	0
Quarter page,	. .	0	6	0
One-eighth page,	. .	0	3	6
Three lines,	. .	0	1	0

Advertisements must reach the *Treasury* Office not later than the 20th of each month.

NOTICE.

All Advertisements appear in the "Musical Star" *and* "Musical Treasury."

As both journals have a large and increasing circulation, advertisers can hardly fail to appreciate the advantages offered by the "Star" *and* "Treasury" *as advertising mediums, only one charge being made.*

The "Musical Star" *and* "Musical Treasury" *may be obtained through all Booksellers and Newsagents, or from the Office, 11 North Bridge, Edinburgh.*

BELLS.

ARTEMUS WARD, having upon one occasion stated a most abstruse and at the same time ridiculous problem to a London cabman with the object of confusing him and enjoying his confusion, was met by the query, "Now, then, guv'nor, don't you think that's rather a dry subject?" There's a good deal to be said on both sides." The same may with much propriety be said of the subject of this article, at least in so far as the abundance of controversial material is concerned. Our literature abounds with references to bells, the poets naturally and as matter of course dealing with bells in their pleasantest connections. Is it of. the Sabbath bells they speak?—they are "sweetly calling unto prayer." Do they wish to convey to our minds the hilarity of a party?—then "all went merry as a marriage bell;" or to inspire us with thoughts of the exhilarating delights of sleighing?—then the sleigh-bells "tinkle, tinkle, tinkle in the icy air of night." We are not unmindful that the poets also keep in mind the more sombre and mournful occasions in which bells are brought into requisition, nor do we forget that the "wild tocsin" appears in effective verse, but probably the bells are referred to more frequently in their joyous than in their sorrowful associations. It is not our purpose in this short sketch to treat of bells either from the poetical point of view or from the point of view of those who regard bells of every size, colour, and tone as an unmitigated evil, but to endeavour to preserve an even balance in the matter. Church bells, being more particularly concerned with the public weal and the public woe, naturally demand our first consideration. From our childhood we have been accustomed to regard a bell as an almost indispensable portion of ecclesiastical equipment. Most of us can recall a youthful period at which we were disinclined to admit the claim of a building to the name of church

which did not possess a bell of some description. Probably many people will be of opinion that the present proportion of churches without bells is by no means too large. In country districts, church bells, rung at regular times, have for generations been of great usefulness. The ringer of the church bell is in some villages regarded, and justly regarded, as a public benefactor. Does he not leave his cosy bed at an early hour in all sorts of weather to announce to the working people of the district the approach of the hours of work, and is there not a sense of satisfaction when in the summer evenings the eight o'clock curfew intimates that there are still some hours of leisure in store for the villagers? Apart from this utilitarian point of view, however, there is a solemn peacefulness about the church bell as its chime reaches us across the meadow on a summer morning, or as it calls the worshippers to service in the quiet evening hours. This indeed seems to us to be the most fitting mission of the church bell. Were it not that it is usually the only available alarm in the country, it would certainly be released from its incongruous duties of announcing indiscriminately a fire or a meeting of heritors! We in Scotland have hitherto been served principally, though not exclusively, by the single bell, while in England chimes are preferred, and consequently much more common. Here is a point in regard to which we may, like Artemus Ward's cabman, remark that there is a good deal to be said on both sides. The manipulation by skilled ringers of a really good peal of bells, say in a suburban district of London on a quiet evening, produces what we are inclined to regard as the perfection of bell music.

We have thus dealt in a general way with what may be called the more agreeable aspects of the subject. We cannot overlook the fact that there are other views which probably deserve as much attention as those we have stated. In towns we not infrequently meet with people who entertain out-and-out abolitionist views in regard to bells. If they had their will, bells of every description would be ruthlessly rooted out from the midst of the community. All of us feel at times the abolitionist spirit upon us, for is not Solomon's dictum that "there is a time for everything" often absolutely ignored? Many of those who have charge of bells have an unhappy knack of fixing upon the wrong time for their performances. We have in our mind a certain London street in which an ardent campanologist persists in playing "Abide with me," and other suitable melodies for hours on end, and that in spite of emphatic neighbourly remonstrances. Again, it is all very well to ring in the New Year, but when your church is situated in a populous locality in which probably there are not a few sick people, it becomes a question whether the sentimental ought not to give way to the practical. It may be doubted whether a church situated among rows of houses is quite the place for musical bells, and yet do we not continually hear in such a situation the notes chasing each other up and down the scale, the reverberations caused by the proximity of the house rendering the sounds well-nigh insupportable. Some bells, too, which are meant to be musical, are nothing more than a miserable jingle. In towns, the single bell is probably on the whole the more tolerable as bells go. At the same time it can scarcely be said that this is a comfort to the hater of bells. No one who has lived in Edinburgh can have failed to hear the frightfully unmusical effects produced by single bells at a little distance from one another. There is no doubt but that in some districts they have constituted themselves a nuisance which ought to be got rid of. It has often struck us that the best way out of the difficulty would be to have a really good resounding bell for each district, which should serve all the churches. The time of day is past which required frequent daily bell-ringing.

An amusing episode occurred last month in the Glasgow Town-Council, the occasion being a recommendation that the salary of the bell-ringer in Blackfriars church should be increased from the munificent yearly £10 to £12 in consideration of the fact that the artist also played the chimes in the church spire! One councillor described the music as "unpleasant," and thought the young man should be dissuaded from attempting hymn-tunes on a chime of five bells! A bailie suggested that the councillor's ear was deficient, whereupon that gentleman vindicated his musical character. Another bailie said they could not expect a fine tune for £12. He thought the man was playing up to his wage. This latter idea was too much for the grave assembly, which consequently relieved itself with a hearty laugh; but the whole discussion, which ended in the preservation of the *status quo,* only proved how true it was that a "good deal could be said on both sides."

The Letter=Box.

A TONIC SOL-FA COLLEGE FOR SCOTLAND.

EDINBURGH, 15th Sept., 1885.

SIR,—Seeing you have solicited an expression of opinion regarding the desirability of establishing a Tonic Sol-fa College for Scotland, I venture to offer a few remarks thereanent. There cannot be the slightest doubt that but for the introduction of the tonic sol-fa system, the knowledge of music would have been much less generally diffused in Scotland than it happily is at the present time. In numerous rural districts, up to quite a recent date, there was comparatively little interest shown in the study of music, in consequence of the difficulty experienced in mastering the technicalities of the old notation, added to the fact that few persons located in such districts had then the necessary knowledge combined with the faculty for lucidly explaining the principles of music to the average rustic mind. The new notation has quite revolutionised this state of affairs, being now eagerly studied by large numbers of our country cousins.

It certainly seems absurd to think that, with such a good work going on in Scotland, we should still require to go across the Border for our certificates of merit; and I trust the proposal you have now put forward will be taken up heartily and energetically until that anomaly ceases to exist, and we have our own Tonic Sol-fa College. Scotland—usually in the van—seems to be wofully behind in matters musical. Even although we have a Professor and a College of Music attached to our University, yet degrees cannot be conferred upon the students who attend until they also pass an examination in England or Ireland. Surely in sol-fa matters we could beat this sham college, at least in some respects!

I would suggest that, before any meeting is held or any action taken, the subject should be thoroughly well ventilated, through the medium of your admirable paper, by the free expression of opinion. A great deal will be gained if correspondents will study moderation of language and avoid personalities and recrimination, as these only prevent the great bulk of ordinary readers from perusing an otherwise useful discussion.

It seems to me the chief obstacle in the way will be the rooting out of the prejudices and petty jealousies of the numerous sections into which those who might combine for such a useful purpose are divided—upon such matters as the scope of the college, and even as to its location. The former, of course, would be subject for debate at a meeting convened for that object; and as to the latter, I cannot conclude without suggesting that Edinburgh would be a most suitable centre for the establishment of such a college. Most institutions nowadays require a paper or journal to convey to the general public a record of the work engaged in and the results obtained; and I am certain it would be most desirable and beneficial to incorporate such particulars within the *Musical Treasury* and *Star,* which have already such a wide-spread and well-deserved circulation.

Do-RAY-ME.

GLASGOW, Sept. 15, 1885.

DEAR SIR,—I am very pleased to see such a lively discussion in the *Treasury* over the proposal to establish a Tonic Sol-fa College north of the Border. I think the proposal is good, and the sooner it is given effect to the better for Scotland. Every such effort must tend to do good, and should be very cordially welcomed by every genuine solfaist.

Why "Musicus" should have been thrown into such a naughty fright over it one can only guess "Musicus" has long ago ceased to have any influence in musical circles here, and his clumsy and selfish efforts to pose as an authority in teaching music are rated by your correspondents at their true value. Do not let the cause of progress suffer because some fossilised stick-in-the-mud has become alarmed lest his craft should be endangered by this movement.

Glasgow is not such a hot-bed of these gentry as your Galashiels correspondent seems to think. There are more men in Glasgow than "Musicus"—men who have quite as good a claim to be heard, and who know more about teaching and notation than he with all his sneers at the lessons in the *Treasury.* I do not wish to be held as sympathising in the least with the views "Musicus" gave expression to, and beg to assure you that I, at least, shall be very pleased to see such a college established soon for the benefit of musical students and for the good of sol-fa.—I am, &c.,

A GLASGOW TEACHER.

EDINBURGH, 14th Sept., 1885.

SIR,—On page 8 of the *Musical Treasury* for September, there appears an article advocating the establishment of a Tonic Sol-fa College for Scotland. In that article every effort is made to convey the impression that the Tonic Sol-fa College, London, is an exclusively "English" institution. Nothing could be further from the truth. Like our Army, Navy, Postal Service, Parliament, &c., it is British, though its headquarters are in London; hence the writer in the *Treasury* betrays either great ignorance or an intention to willfully mislead his readers. It can hardly be ignorance, so, in the belief that it is misrepresentation, I may remark that Tonic Sol-faists, as a class, are too intelligent to be hoodwinked so easily; and it may be safely predicted that any attempt, by such questionable means, to establish a *rival* College to that in whose solid worth they have justly so much confidence will utterly fail.

After a sentence, in which the writer gets considerably "mixed" in regard to "notation" and "music," not seeming to be aware that they are different things, he begins his second paragraph by saying—"*As most of our readers know, our English neighbours are in advance of us in the matter of high-class tonic sol-fa education.*" This may be met by the counter statement that, probably "most of our readers know" the very reverse to be the case—namely, that in proportion to the number of its inhabitants, Scotland possesses more highly-educated tonic sol-faists than England and Ireland taken together.

That there is some inconvenience caused to Scottish tonic sol-fa students by their College being in London, may be admitted; but this could be obviated, and the whole question solved, by forming branches of the parent College wherever it might be practicable.

To the late lamented John Curwen there were neither English, Irish, nor Scotchmen; there were only his fellow-men whom he wished to benefit. So it comes to-day that "The Tonic Sol-fa College for the People," the founding of which was the crowning achievement of his life, is open to all on equal terms, without distinction of race, country, colour, or creed. Therefore, to speak of the Tonic Sol-fa College as being "English," is as unjust as it is ungenerous—at once an outrage upon truth and a libel on the memory of a truly philanthropic and noble-minded man.

Trusting that these remarks may recall the true state of the case to the minds of such tonic-sol-faists as may have forgotten it—if any such there be,—I am, Sir, &c.,
THOS. YOUNG.

EDINBURGH, 10th Sept., 1885.

SIR,—The proposal now being ventilated through your columns to establish a Tonic Sol-fa College in Scotland, will never come to anything. I am positively certain of this. The reasons are not far to seek. Any proposal or suggestion—it matters not a jot how disinterestedly it is made—having reference to sol-fa matters, emanating from Edinburgh, will not be supported, or even countenanced, by the great men of Glasgow. On the other hand, they will strive with might and main to ignominiously crush any scheme that is set afoot; and they will do this without giving the slightest consideration to the fact that such scheme might do a vast amount of good to promote the interests and welfare of the sol-fa movement. It is well enough known that there is no profession under the sun where more blind jealousy exists than in the musical profession; and while this applies to musicians of all types and classes, the evil is seen at its very worst amongst those who are connected with the tonic sol-fa. I state this fearlessly and challenge contradiction. Any such proposal, therefore, I believe to be altogether out of the question, more particularly as it comes from the Metropolis. Glasgow sol-faists have a very poor opinion of their brethren in Edinburgh; and though they will cheerfully submit to be led by the nose by any other town or institution outside their own country, they would make any sacrifice rather than co-operate with their friends in the capital—no matter how great the benefit to them might be.

You will no doubt receive the support of a certain section of sol-faists who are wise enough to see that Scotland is ripe for something more substantial than a branch of an English college; but as that section, I am afraid, will be small in number, it will not go for much. I would fain wish you success, but the case is too hopeless.—Yours, &c.,
JARVIS.

EDINBURGH, 25th Sept., 1885.

SIR,—I have read with interest your short articles, and the letters which they have called forth, in reference to the provision of a Tonic Sol-fa College for Scotland. I am always pleased to see anything which has for its end our improvement in matters musical, and I feel certain no one will regret the discussion in your columns. Perhaps you will allow me to say, however, that I think the present College in England meets all the requirements of the case. If there were anything distinctive in Scottish tonic sol-fa, as compared with English sol-fa, then there might be some reason for the founding of an institution which should bear testimony to our national characteristics; but, seeing that sol-fa is sol-fa and nothing else, why should we bother about rearing an institution which would merely do what the English College is at present efficiently doing, *i.e.*, putting its students through a course of training, and then permitting them to affix four letters to their names. So far as the sending of cash across the Border is concerned, I think we need not vex ourselves much about it. Tonic sol-faists are certainly a very enthusiastic class of people, but I am inclined to advise them to temper their zeal with discretion. If it were resolved to have a Tonic Sol-fa College for Scotland, sol-faists would require to be prepared to thrust their hands into their pockets to some purpose, unless they were content to merely rent a room in some of the less brilliant parts of the City in which to carry on collegiate operations. To put the Quaker question—" Do the sol-faists sympathise £20 each or so?"—Yours, &c.,
MUSICUS No. 2.

6 TANNADICE ST., DUNDEE, 10th Sept., 1885.

DEAR SIR,—I was very sorry at reading the correspondence in this month's *Treasury*, anent the opening of an Edinburgh College for the propagation of tonic sol-fa, to find that Mr. J. C. Grieve had been very unwarrantably brought into the correspondence. But doubly sorry was I that men talented to write such letters would waste such an amount of paper, ink, and time—that most valuable adjunct of all—in running down such a novice as the one who styles himself "Musicus" must be. Let us live the like of him down. First, as to Mr. J. C. Grieve; he is a man I have had correspondence with, but never saw. He has done me so much good, however, that, should I ever meet him, I shall at least shake him most warmly by the hand. I have written the tests which "Musicus" has taken upon himself to call confusion, and have found them very beneficial confusion indeed.

But, Mr. Editor, we want proposals for the working of our Scottish College, and not for the confounding of an ignoramus. I would not have the thing hurriedly gone into, but have all points considered. Would it not be better to include staff notation as well? Would it not also be as well to have all sorts of instrumental music wrought up? These, and many others, are points well worthy our attention, and will better repay us.—Truly yours,
BRIMBORIAM.

The following letters appeared in the *Glasgow Mail*:—

TONIC SOL-FA COLLEGE FOR SCOTLAND.

SIR,—In my last letter it appears I have most unwittingly and unintentionally given offence to a gentleman in Edinburgh, whose name I did not even know. There is not a syllable personal to any one in my letter ; I merely offered, as requested, some suggestions in reference to an article in the *Musical Treasury*, for which publication I only knew the editor as responsible. Why this should have brought down upon me such a severe personal attack I really cannot imagine. No exception is taken to my remarks upon the proposal contained in this article, and all that I have said in reference to the "new notation" is admitted by Mr. Grieve, but he adds that what I complain of is "intentional." I highly approve of musical problems being submitted for solution, but I hold very strongly that all such should be set in a musical manner, so that they can be sung and resolved correctly. Neither of these requirements can be applied to those at page 15 of the *Treasury*. They are intended to embrace the niceties of the enharmonic scale, though these are frequently used in a very peculiar manner, but they can only be even apparently resolved by using all the imperfections of the tempered scale. This, I need hardly say, is no true musical solution, but destroys the problem altogether. It is, further, very confusing to the student, leading to the idea that the enharmonic and tempered scales are convertible. If so, why trouble them with the enharmonic scale at all? I am very pleased to see attention called to the niceties of musical notation. Nothing has so hindered the progress of vocal music as imperfect notation and illegitimate transition, the necessary and constant causes of the rough singing and falling in pitch so destructive to our choral music.—I am, &c.,   MUSICUS.
Aug. 19.

SIR,—"Musicus" in his second letter says I admitted in my last all that he said in his first letter. I scarcely think I did. However, I cannot admit all that he says in his later epistle. He asserts that the examples on page 15 of the *Treasury* are not set in a musical manner, as they can neither be sung nor resolved properly ; and he makes some remarks upon the niceties of the enharmonic scale in such a general way as may be taken to mean anything or nothing, just as one chooses. What, I would ask, has the enharmonic scale to do with the examples, as examples? They are written in tonic sol-fa notation (at least, they are supposed to be), and that notation—nor, indeed, any notation under the sun—cannot depict properly the niceties of the enharmonic, nor yet of the chromatic—no, nor even of the diatonic scale correctly. Certain niceties of intonation are often implied in the tonic sol-fa, as well as in other notations, although they are not definitely expressed ; and I hold that the notation of the tests is as conformable to tonic sol-fa principles as to write t l s in a cadence transition when m r d are the actual sounds represented. As to the tests not being singable, that will depend on the singer. The exactness of the sounds produced by the singer does not depend upon whether the notes are named m fe or m bah, but upon the perception and appreciation of the vocalist concerning the interval he is required to produce, and his ability to produce it. "The imperfections of the tempered scale," which "Musicus" says are necessary for the proper resolution of the tests, have really nothing to do in the matter. How these "imperfections" are to be employed in the resolution is a kind of a puzzle, as the notation cannot represent them, and it is

only by means of the notation that the resolution is to be arrived at. "The imperfections of the tempered scale" can only exist in the imagination, so to speak. of any one looking at a piece of tonic sol-fa music ; and the nature of these "imperfections" will depend on the individual interpretation put upon the sol-fa syllables. I maintain that the tests are not only practical, but that they are scientifically correct. Had this been a musical journal I would have sent you a minute analysis of the tests complained of, showing that no tempered intervals are necessary for their proper solution, but that every interval employed may be strictly in accordance with just intonation. I thoroughly agree with "Musicus" in his concluding sentence, that "imperfect notation and illegitimate transition" have seriously "hindered the cause of vocal music ;" and I would only add it is for the very purpose of enabling students to understand those imperfections and illegitimacies that the *Treasury* test problems are partly designed.—I am, &c.,   JOHN C. GRIEVE.
8 Rankeillor Street, Edinburgh, Aug. 24.

AN EVENING AT CHOPIN'S.

IT is about nine o'clock in the evening. Chopin is seated at the piano, the room is dimly lighted by a few waxcandles. Several men of brilliant renown are grouped in the luminous zone immediately around the piano.

Heine, the sad humorist, leans over his shoulder, and as the tapering fingers wander meditatively over the ivory keys, asks "if the trees at moonlight sang always so harmoniously?"

Meyerbeer is seated by his side ; his grave and thoughtful head moves at times with a tacit acquiescence and delight, and he almost forgets the ring of his own Cyclopæan harmonies in listening to the delicate Arabesque-woven mazourkas of his friend.

Adolphe Nourrit, the noble and ascetic artist, stands apart. He has something of the grandeur of the Middle Ages about him. In his later years he refused to paint any subject which was wanting in true dignity. Like Chopin he served art with a severe exclusiveness and a passionate devotion.

Eugene Delacroix leans against the piano, absorbed in meditation—developing, it may be, in his own mind, some form of beauty, or some splendid tint, suggested by the strange analogies which exist between sound and colour.

Buried in a fauteuil, with her arms resting on a table, sat Madame Sand, curiously attentive, gracefully subdued. She is listening to the language of the emotions—fascinated by the subtle gradations of thought and feelings which she herself delighted to express. It is in memory of some such golden hours that she writes :—"There is no mightier art than this to awaken in man the sublime consciousness of his own humanity—to paint before his mind's eye the rich splendours of nature—the joy of meditation—the national character of a people—the passionate tumult of their hopes and fears—the languor and despondency of their sufferings. Remorse, violence, terror, control, despair, enthusiasm, faith, disquietude, glory, calm—these and a thousand other nameless emotions belong to music. Without stooping to a puerile imitation of noises and effects, she transports us in the spirit to strange and distant scenes. There we wander to and fro in the dim air, and, like Æneas in the Elysian fields, all we behold is greater than on earth—godlike, changed, idealised."

    .   .   .   .   .

One evening towards sunset, Chopin, who had lain insensible for many hours, suddenly rallied. He observed the Countess draped in white standing at the foot of the bed. She was weeping bitterly. "Sing!" murmured the dying man. She had a lovely voice. It was a strange request, but so earnest a one that his friends wheeled the piano from the adjoining parlour to his bedroom door, and there, as the twilight deepened, with the last rays of the setting sun streaming into the room, the Countess sang that famous canticle to the Virgin, which it is said once saved the life of Stradella. "How beautiful it is!" he exclaimed; "My God, how beautiful! Again, again!" In another moment he swooned away.—*H. R. Harris.*

MECHANICAL STREET MUSIC.

It is commonly believed that street-organs, hurdy-gurdies, and kindred instruments are looked upon with particular dislike by all orthodox musicians. It appears, however, that the common belief is an inaccurate one. In 1861 the celebrated advocate, Adolphe Crémieux, was engaged to plead the cause of certain organ-grinders who were indicted in Paris as public nuisances; and, in order to obtain materials for the defence, he applied to three of the leading composers of the day for their opinions about street-organs and hurdy-gurdies. Two of the replies have recently been discovered among a large collection of autographs that was left by the great lawyer, and the letters are printed in the current number of the *Revue Politique et Littéraire.* J. F. Halévy wrote :—"I do not believe that any composer will admit that his reputation suffers when a few of his melodies are reproduced on the street-organs and other musical boxes to which you allude; I believe, on the contrary, that airs which are thus made public not only do not lessen the reputation of the composer, but give it an additional popularity which is not unwelcome. Of course, the composer likes great singers—celebrated tenors and illustrious prima donnas—yet there is good in the *vox populi*, and he is far from despising it." Rossini was next appealed to, but his reply is not given. It was evidently much to the same effect as Halévy's, for Auber, who was the third composer to whom the question was referred, wrote :—"I entirely agree with Rossini and Halévy, and I beg to add my testimony to theirs. The success of the street is not the least flattering of all." Not one of these distinguished musicians went so far as to declare that the strains of a hand-organ were soothing to him, or that he had an active liking for the lugubrious outpourings of a hurdy-gurdy; and therefore it may not be æsthetically incumbent upon a mere every-day lover of music to go into raptures whenever Giovanni Giovanelli elects to churn out discordant fragments of opera within hearing. It may be added that the composers of the advanced school, writing with a sublime contempt for, or neglect of melody, are not likely to suffer from "grinding," or to gain popularity after this manner.

APPOINTMENTS.

Mr. John M'Laren, leader of psalmody in St. Brycedale Free Church, has been appointed teacher of music under Kingborn School Board.

Mr. William G. Dunsmore (late of Holyrood F. C.), has been elected precentor of Campbeltown U. P. Church. After hearing a leet, which were chosen out of the twenty-eight applications sent in, the precentor's Committee gave in their report at a meeting held for that purpose. Ex-Provost Greenlees moved, and Mr. A. Colville seconded, that Mr. W. G. Dunsmore, of Edinburgh, be elected precentor. The motion was put and carried unanimously.

A Hint for Pianists.—A foreign medical man counsels those who practise frequently on the piano, harp, and stringed instruments generally, to submit to a surgical operation, which consists in dividing the tendon of the annulary or ring-finger. Pianists are aware that, out of the five fingers composing the hand, the fourth one, as it is termed, is the most rebellious in action, being alike the weakest and least flexible of all the others. This feebleness proceeds from the lateral tendons that join the annulary to the other fingers, and in a measure paralyses its movements. It seems that the operation is not painful, the patient loses but little blood, and the fingers become as free as the others, and can work upon the key-board or music-strings with equal force and facility.

Negro Festivities.—Negro festivities, as represented on the stage, are cheerful and jovial proceedings, replete with fun and good temper; but in sober reality they are not unfrequently scenes of disputes and bloodshed. The negroes carry knives and razors, and use them on the slightest provocation, and "desperate frays at negro gatherings" is a stock heading in American journals. It is not often, however, that the cause of dispute is as slight as that which set the "sons and daughters of Moab" by the ears at a picnic near Richmond, Virginia. The trouble had its origin in a misunderstanding about which tune the brass band should play. Anthony and some of his friends insisted it should be "Wait till the clouds roll by." Another faction demanded a livelier air, called "Dancing Jimmy." The two factions became greatly excited, and in the melee a dozen razors were flashed in the sunlight. A coloured constable on the ground arrested the fighters. Anthony attempted to rescue his friends from the officers. The constable, after repeated warnings, drew an old, rusty, pepperbox revolver, and shot him. Several other men were severely wounded in the fray. The negro has always been fond of music, but it would hardly have been thought that whether "Wait till the clouds roll by" or "Dancing Jimmy" should be played first was a question of sufficient importance to cause a score of sober enthusiasts to go at each other's throats with deadly weapons.

General Grant and Music.—Amongst other reminiscences of the late General Grant is one concerning his singularly intense dislike for music. Many persons do not care for music; others only like certain kinds of music; but General Grant positively detested it in any and every form. The narrator who recalls this curious trait in his character remarks that, when Marshal MacMahon was President of the French Republic, he had frequently an opportunity of seeing the patient endurance of the American hero put to a severe test. Being on a visit to the French capital, the Marshal used often to place the Presidential box at the Grand Opera at his disposal, and etiquette prevented him from declining the proffered courtesy. He could not stay away, but what he endured, we are told, in the cause of politeness on such occasions can best be understood by those who knew him intimately. He would sit passively enduring what to him was real suffering throughout an opera; not a muscle of his face would change or betray him; but afterwards he would confess to a friend the reality of the sufferings he had undergone. His dislike for music also caused him real inconvenience when in society. Those who knew of it took care that if the General was at a "soiree" there should be neither singing nor piano-playing; but in many instances his host and hostess were unacquainted with this peculiarity, and amateur vocalists and pianists would insist on performing for his benefit. His answer to "What shall I sing, or what shall I play to you, General?" in such cases was the discouraging one, "Something short."

New Music.

J. WIGHTMAN & SON, 13 South Castle Street, Edinburgh.
My Harp is upon the Willow. Sacred Song. Words by Newton. Composed by W. P. Gale. Price 2s. Although sacred songs are not in great demand in the musical market, a composition of this class, with any claim to merit, rarely fails to secure a fair measure of success. *My Harp is upon the Willow,* the composer of which is known in Edinburgh as a clever organist and choirmaster, is distinguished by a melody and harmony that are at once simple and effective. Mr. Gale has been especially happy in the selection of his words, and displays excellent taste and unmistakable ability in their treatment. Key E flat; compass B flat to E.

T. H. BARNETT, 40 Poland Street, London, W.
The Finished Song. Words by R. Sydney. Composed by Orsino Salari. Price 2s. An admirable song with a pleasing melody and highly elaborate, if somewhat heavy, accompaniment. The words are of more than average merit. Two keys—E flat and F.

C. B. TREE, 132 Petherton Road, Highbury, New Park, London.
Our Darling. Song. Words by Ray Lotinga. Composed by Lindsay Proctor. Price 2s. There is a simple pathos in this pretty little ballad that should make it popular. Three keys—F, G, and B flat; compass B flat to D.

OSBORN & TUCKWOOD, 64 Berners Street, London, W.
The Vesper Voluntaries for Organ, Harmonium, or American Organ. Book Seven of this series is assuredly one of the best shilling's worth offered to the public in this age of cheap music. Young organists and harmoniumists will find in this number many beautifully harmonised themes that are really a pleasure to play. The book deserves a large sale.—*Drucie : Dance for the Pianoforte.* Price 1s. 6d. By A. J. Carpenter. An easy and tuneful, if not very original piece.—*The Freebooter.* Song. Words by Lindsay Lennox. Composed by Morton Elliott. Price 2s. net. The composer has been successful in hitting off the rollicking joviality which is generally associated with members of the "freebooter" fraternity. It is a capital song for a baritone. Two keys—F and E flat; compass C to F or D.—*Danse Entrancing.* Composed by E. Boggetti. A sprightly and pleasing piano sketch. It is not at all difficult, and being extremely "catchy," it is just the sort of piece to attract and interest young executants.—*Pug Polka.* Price 2s. By the same composer, is somewhat unequal, but the trio movement is bright and pretty. The frontispiece is neatly illustrated.—*Once in a While.* Song. Words by G. Clifton Bingham. Composed by Arthur J. Greenish. Price 2s. The fashion set by the popularity of *Same Day* has induced many song-writers to imitate, with more or less success, this style of drawing-room ditty. *Once in a While* is a charming example of this class, the melody being fresh, and the accompaniment uncommonly good. There is a violin obbligato. Two keys—C and A; compass G to F.

GEORGE ELLIOTT KENT, Askern, Doncaster.
Britannia's Heroes of the Nile. Written and composed by George Elliott Kent. Price 2s. There is an appalling recklessness about the following lines (which are a fair specimen of the words of this patriotic song) that cannot fail to satisfy the most sanguinary jingo :—

> Let Hicks and Gordon be your cry;
> Bravo British heroes to Khartoum hie:
> Tho' death and hell before you lay.
> There Britain's flag must float to-day,
> Tho' reek and blood fill up the way.

The music is appropriately vigorous and spirited. Key A; compass E to D.

HENRY KLEIN, 3 Holborn Viaduct, London, E.C.
Pauline Lucca Waltz. Price 2s. *Botschafter (Ambassador) Waltz.* Price 2s. By Henry Klein. These two sets of waltzes are excellent examples of this prolific composer's best workmanship. Both are admirable dance measures, and possess considerable musical interest.—*The Last Muster.* Song. Words by Juba Kennerley. Composed by Henry Pontet. Price 2s. There is genuine artistic beauty both in words and music of this song. The former belong to the best class of song poetry, and Mr. Pontet has dealt with them in a manner well worthy of his reputation as an accomplished and skilful musician. There is an *ad lib.* harmonium accompaniment. Three keys—B flat, C and E flat; compass, B flat to D.—*Earth's Secret.* Song. Words and Music by Oonagh. Price 2s. Simplicity and prettiness are the chief features in this petit ballad. Key B flat; compass E to G.

Musical Gossip.

New music, and matters of interest for notice in this column, should be addressed, EDITOR, *Musical Treasury,* 11 N. Bridge, Edinburgh.

ON Friday, the 28th August, the members of Woodside Church Choir, Glasgow, met and presented Mr. J. Clapperton with a handsome epergne, as a token of the high esteem in which he was held by them, and as a mark of their appreciation of his services in the capacity of organist and choirmaster of Woodside Church. Mr. Wilson, in a few words, made the presentation. Mr. Clapperton replied in suitable terms, and thereafter a pleasant and harmonious evening was spent. Mr. Clapperton (who was recently appointed organist of Sandyford Church) has also been elected to Belmont Established Church, the duties of which he will carry on in addition to those of Sandyford.

THE Glasgow St. Andrew's Musical Association, under its clever conductor, Mr. D. S. Allan, will shortly be in full swing, and is even now engaged in weekly rehearsals. During the coming season, this Society will, judging from its scheme, not only sustain, but add to, the high reputation won in past years. Strong in membership, with many first class voices, and led by the beat of so able a conductor as Mr. Allan, much good work may be anticipated.

AFTER the presentation in Dublin to Madame Marie Rose of a gold bracelet by Major Macfarlane and twenty-three ladies and gentlemen of the Irish capital, the crowd outside wished to draw the *prima donna's* carriage to the hotel, and in the struggle somebody purloined a silver cigarette case out of Colonel Henry Mapleson's side pocket. There is something like a precedent for this, as it seems when the Dublin crowd wished to drag the late Mdlle. Titiens home in triumph, the horses were never returned, and Lieut.-Colonel J. H. Mapleson and Titiens had subsequently to arrange the matter with the prosaic livery stable-keeper.

Ibonourable Mention Certificate.

TEST NO. 5 *(New Notation).*

a. Construct as many common chords, in various positions, as you can, using r in the key of C as the bass note in every case.

b. Harmonise the following bass, making f ur-part harmony; no note shorter than *one* pulse to be used in the added parts:—

Key B flat.

{ d₁	: s₁	d .t₁,l₁ : s₁f₁f₁t₁	d₁ .r₁f₁ : f₁s₁ f₁f₁		
{ r₁	.f₁ ,f₁ : s₁ ,l₁ .s₁ ,f₁	f₁	.f₁ ,s₁ : l₁ ,t₁ .l₁ ,s₁		
{ f₁r₁f₁f₁ : s₁ s₂	d₁	—	— :	||

c. Tell what keys the chords in requirement *a* would be D, or *L* chords of.

a. Key E.   SOLUTION OF TEST NO. 4.

{ .s	d .m : s ,fe	s ,re : m ,t₁	d .r : m .f		
{ s .m f : s l f	s .l ,t : d¹r¹t	d¹	:— .d¹		
{ f .l : d¹ ,t	d¹ ,se : l ,m	f .s : l .ta		
{ d.l,ta : d¹,r.ta	d¹,d¹ : d¹,s,l,t	d¹ .t,l : s,f,m,r	d : — .	

b. Key E flat.   1.———   2.———

{ d	d : m,f s : m	d¹ : t	l	l : s.t.d¹	r¹ : t	s : m	r ||

3.———   4.———

{ r	r : m,f m : s	f : m	r	r	m : f.s	l : f	m : r	d ||

1. Cadence modulation.
2. Transition to the dominant of the first sharp key.
3. Extended transitional modulation.
4. Passing transition to the sub-dominant of the original key.

c. Key E flat.   B flat. t.

{ d	d : m,f s : m	d¹ : t	l	¹r	d : m,f s : m	d : l₁ s₁ ||

d. f. A flat.   *LAH* is *F.*   E flat. t.   f. A flat.   E flat. t.

{ ᵗl₁| l₁ : t,d	t₁:r	d : t₁	l₁	¹r : ᶠd,r	ᵘl¹:f	m : r	d ||

The following is the explanation of a few points wherein some of the test-papers were wrong:—

In the first line of the *test* this passage occurs:—

re | m ,t₁ : d .,se₁ | l₁

Divested of what we may consider its embellishments, the passage would stand plainly thus: | m : d | l₁ the o being the three notes of the minor chord. Each of the notes is approached in the *test* by a semitone from below. The notes of approach being *quarter-pulse* tones, may be considered as non-essential; they are, in fact, *incidental guiding* notes, or mele tic leading notes, directing the ear to the three principal notes already mentioned, m .d .l₁. In the *major*, the parallel passage to m ,d ,l₁ is s .m .d; and if we ornament this latter passage similar to the minor passage in the *test*, the result should be what we have given in the above *solution* at *a*. There is another point. The ta's given in our *solution* were, in most of the papers, set down as t's; this is wrong. The *test* is written in the "improper method." Had it been put in the "better method," the key would have been changed at the last note of the second line, thus: C. *LAH* is *A*;   because if twenty notes are taken in succession, beginning at this point, they will be found to be the very same in effect, and in relation, as the first twenty notes of the *test*; showing that the first passage of twenty notes is repeated further on in another key. If the *test* were written in the "better method," the fourth last measure, for example, would appear thus: | m .d ,r : m .f ,r | m, and the *major* parallel would be this: | s .m ,f : s .| ,f | s; in the improper method the above extract appears in the *test* thus: | l .f ,s : l .s | l, and its *major* parallel should appear in the *solution* as we have given it.

Several of the candidates mentioned that they did not know exactly how to work the *b* requirement, being puzzled as to how to make the necessary changes of key without using accidentals. Seeing that it was only the *melody* of the psalm-tune that was to be written, it need only be explained that th key may change without any of the *distinguishing tones* appearing in the melody. In the *solution* of this requirement, as given above, none of the distin-

guishing tones *appear* in the melody, but they are nevertheless *implied*, and would, of course, be introduced, if the melody were harmonised, in some of the parts.

J. C. G.

PASS LIST.

Corresponding Class.

For conditions, see "Star" for October, 1884.

FIRST COURSE—HARMONY.

Text-book—Novello's Music Primer, "Harmony," by Dr. Stainer.

LESSON XIII.

Chap. X., page 76. Study pars. 116-118, with intervening examples.

Note.—In par. 116 we are told that the suspension 4 to 3 is rarely found on the sub-dominant and leading note. It is much more frequently employed on the sub-dominant than on the leading note. Stainer says the reason it is rarely used on the sub-dominant is because the fourth from the sub-dominant is an augmented fourth; this, in my opinion, is no valid objection, as the fourth, being augmented, and also by reason of its incisive character as the leading note, only renders the discord more piquant. The percussion and the resolution of the suspended fourth on the sub-dominant produce a strong and effective contrast of pungency and sweetness which cannot be so effectively and so simply obtained by any other means. Here is a common instance of the suspended fourth on the sub-dominant:—

The suspended fourth on the leading note has less to recommend it, as the resolution must be effected on the chord of the leading note, which is not a completely consonant chord. The contrast between the *percussion* and the *resolution* of the suspended fourth on the leading note is not so great as in the previous example, neither is the result so satisfactory as in most other suspensions; nevertheless, it might be employed thus:—

The pupil is not advised to employ this, unless it be in a sequence.

Exercise.—Instead of doing the exercise given after par. 118, write 4 to 3 suspensions on every note of the scale, in the key of D.

Study par. 119.

Note.—The student may here be a little perplexed. In par. 116 he is told that the 4 to 3 suspension is found on every degree of the scale, and in this par. he is told that when it occurs on the 5th degree of the scale it is not a suspension. This is a trifle paradoxical. Clearly, if the 4 to 3 on the dominant is *prepared*, it is a suspension; because, having a proper *preparation*, *percussion*, and *resolution*, it follows the common rule of all suspensions. When the 4 to 3 on the dominant has no *preparation*, then it may be considered as an individual chord of the dominant eleventh. The dominant eleventh is the dominant ninth with another third superposed. With its full complement of notes it appears thus:—G—B—D—F—A—C. In four-part harmony it usually appears thus:—G—D—G—C, having its root doubled; or thus:—G—D—F—C, having its seventh introduced; in both ways we find the chord employed in Ex. 112, but there the discord C (that is the 4th), being prepared, it must be considered as a properly treated suspension.

Study pars. 120, 121, with intervening examples.

Note.—From the former of these pars. it will easily be discerned that when the note of discord moves up to its resolution it is called a *ritardation*; this is in contradistinction to *suspension*, which the device is called when the dissonant note moves down.

Exercises.—Page 80, No. V.; page 119, No. 79, 82.

Write a L.M. tune introducing 4 to 3 suspensions.

J. C. G.